# A PAGEANT
# TRULY PLAY'D

*For my parents*
*David Blair and Phyllis Rose*

# A PAGEANT TRULY PLAY'D

*Constance Smedley and Maxwell Armfield*
*Writers and Artists*

TESSA WEST

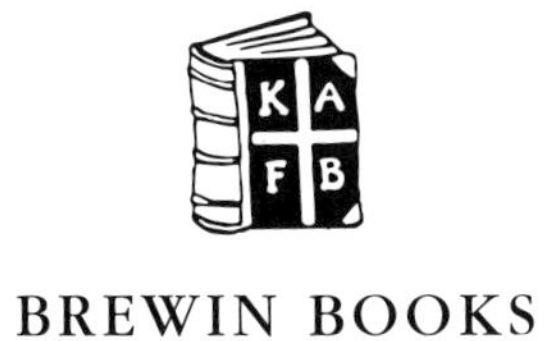

BREWIN BOOKS

BREWIN BOOKS
19 Enfield Ind. Estate,
Redditch,
Worcestershire,
B97 6BY
www.brewinbooks.com

Published by Brewin Books 2020



A CIP catalogue record for this book is
available from the British Library.

ISBN: 978-1-85858-722-6

Printed and bound in Great Britain by
Page Bros Ltd.

# Contents


| | | |
|---|---|---|
| | Acknowledgements | vii |
| | Prologue | viii |
| 1 | Connie and Max | 1 |
| 2 | Pageant | 3 |
| 3 | Connie's Early Life and Family | 5 |
| 4 | David's Beginning | 12 |
| 5 | Max's Childhood and Youth, and Quakerism | 14 |
| 6 | David's Bereavement | 18 |
| 7 | More About Connie | 19 |
| 8 | The Unexpected | 20 |
| 9 | Max's Early Life and Schooldays at Sidcot | 26 |
| 10 | Connie Growing Up in Birmingham | 32 |
| 11 | Ida | 35 |
| 12 | Max Moves to Birmingham | 38 |
| 13 | David's Mother Plans to Return to Scotland | 40 |
| 14 | Connie Embarks on Writing | 42 |
| 15 | Women's Movement | 45 |
| 16 | Politics | 47 |
| 17 | Connie Spreads Her Wings | 49 |
| 18 | Connie Continues Writing | 51 |
| 19 | The Armfields | 55 |
| 20 | David Moves to Scotland | 57 |
| 21 | Max at Birmingham School of Art | 59 |
| 22 | Start of Lyceum | 65 |
| 23 | More About Birmingham | 66 |
| 24 | How Did David and Max Meet? | 67 |
| 25 | David's Activities and Interests in the War Years | 73 |
| 26 | More About Max and His Fellow Students | 77 |
| 27 | Painting in Tempera | 80 |
| 28 | Connie and the Lyceum | 83 |
| 29 | The Lyceum and the Women's Movement | 88 |
| 30 | The Lyceum Opens | 91 |

31  Max in France                                     93
32  Max's Friendships                                 97
33  Connie Appears                                    99
34  Weddings                                          104
35  Country Life and Christian Science                108
36  Making the Pageant                                111
37  The Cotswold Players                              115
38  Post Pageant                                      117
39  Dance Development                                 119
40  Greenleaf Theatre                                 121
41  War Approaches and Move to the U.S.               125
42  Letters Home                                      128
43  Success                                           131
44  Omissions                                         133
45  More About the U.S.                               135
46  Santa Fe                                          137
47  Return to England                                 140
48  Grace Darling                                     143
49  Crusaders                                         144
50  Events in England                                 146
51  Slowing Down                                      148
52  Connie's Last Days                                150
53  David's Ending                                    152
54  David's Letter to His Godson                      154
55  Max's Approach to Art                             156
56  Max on His Own                                    158
57  Occult                                            159
58  Alexander Ballard                                 161
59  A Glimpse Across Constance's Career               163
60  A Glimpse Across Maxwell's Career                 164
61  Max's Last Letters                                166
    Epilogue                                          168
    Appendix 1                                        169
    Appendix 2                                        171
    Appendix 3                                        172
    Bibliography                                      173

# Acknowledgements

My thanks go to a large number of people for their various generous contributions in the form of books and photos, papers and diaries, documents, suggestions, time and cups of tea. It has been busy and I have enjoyed the writing as much as the research, and the making of connections. So, warm thanks to John Allinson, Diana Armfield, Ruth Bradbury, Grace Brockington, Margaret Chaplin, Jane Crawshaw, Ralph Crawshaw, Penny Freedman, Christine Gladwin, Rebecca Guyer, John Hawkins, Marion Jones, Ken McQueen, Claire Mitchell, Suzanne Moreton, Darragh O'Donoghue, Victoria Osbourne, Anne and John Shneerson, Peyton Skipwith, Anne Thomson, Duncan Walker, Fiona Waterhouse and Roger Williamson. And I must not forget four from the Cotswolds: Howard Beard, Sue Freck, Frank Hatt and Patrick Howell.

# Prologue

The names of the couple who are the main subjects of this book are Maxwell Armfield (1881-1972) and Constance Smedley (1876-1941). I came across them when seeking a new subject for a biography. Briefly, one of them was an artist and illustrator, and one was a writer and dramaturge. But those labels do little more than indicate the couple's primary areas of interest and activity. I chose them out of a short list of other possibilities because I could see that they were both unusual, admirable and inspiring people.

As well as having the ability to knuckle down with imagination and skill to the practicalities of creating art work and creating audiences, exhibitions and books, plays and a prestigious club, both of them had a spirit of other-worldliness. Moreover, they also had a desire to contribute to the common good, and to beauty. And, importantly, Constance was active in the women's movement when she was young while Maxwell was already attracting interest in his distinctive paintings. Their contrasting characters and their determination to push boundaries meant that they led unorthodox and often unpredictable lives. They were, separately, already doing those things when they first met, but their marriage in 1909 led to them exploring and developing different art forms. Also relevant to their lives were the facts that Constance was physically disabled from early childhood, and Maxwell was actively gay for at least some of his life.

As my initial research increased in scope and depth, I found I was regarding the pair as a special discovery: an excellent and delightful outcome for any biographer. As I am not an artist nor a playwright, I realised I was perhaps being ambitious in undertaking the task I was setting myself, but the feeling of "rightness" grew and, in the absence (to date, at least) of a conventional biography of either Maxwell or Constance, I decided to write this book to find out about them and the world they lived in, and to celebrate them.

This is not an academic text with abstract discussions, formal footnotes and references, but a book which will, I hope, interest outward-looking readers in these unusual and unsung characters and in what they did in their lives. Max and Connie are not well-known, but I have found that those who knew them or know about them, liked them. I therefore began to track down the raw material that biographers need: articles, correspondence, ephemera, diaries, documents and suppliers of information such as close family members or others whose contact with one or both of the subjects had been important even if fleeting.

Little did I know that right at the beginning of my explorations, something relevant, vital and unknown would present itself out of the blue.

By chance, quite apart from but simultaneously to my first research sorties, I had arranged with my brother Roger to go through a pile of family-related documents, sketches and correspondence that we had paid little attention to before. We already had precious love letters between our parents and some very positive testimonials from senior staff of organisations for whom our father had worked and – quite separately – from those to whom our mother had taught ballroom dancing in the 1920s.

Unexpectedly, as Roger and I leafed through the papers, we came across two small wooden boards, each measuring 22 x 27 centimetres: the size of a small tray. They were paintings, oil on board. Both of them depicted a scene abroad, and carried a title: one was *Fishing Boats at Venice*, the other was *The Citadel, Pisa*. Roger and I liked them both. A signature on the back of each of them made it quite clear that they were painted by Maxwell Ashby Armfield – the artist who was one of the two people I was just beginning to research. We were astonished.

We also found a pencil portrait by Maxwell Armfield of our now deceased father, David Blair Williamson, and beneath the image, in a tiny, neat hand we found the words *"La dove io t'amai prima."* This phrase of Michelangelo's translates as *"There, where I first loved you."* Maxwell Armfield had also written a comment about the likeness of his sketch – he was not entirely satisfied with it. And there was also a small watercolour (dated 1946) of Polperro in Cornwall, painted by David, our father. Roger and I both then gradually recalled the name Maxwell Armfield from early childhood, but we knew nothing about him.

We thought that Maxwell must have given the two paintings to our father in about 1943 or 1944, when, we worked out, the two could have first met each other. There is no evidence of contact until then, and their friendship would end in 1949.

Sitting on the carpet and coming across these pictures caused me both to reflect on my father and to think more deeply about the artist. Who was Maxwell Armfield? How did he and my father know each other? Where did they meet? What was their relationship?

As I carried the paintings home I was full of questions, and knew I would have to extend my research. For a start, I discovered that our newly acquired paintings of Italy had been published in Maxwell's book *An Artist in Italy*. While I had deliberately chosen my subjects Constance and Maxwell with care and thought, it almost felt as if David, my father, an unexpected but very welcome third character, was wanting to join in. This feeling began to work itself deep into my mind and my imagination.

*"A Pageant Truly Play'd"*

William Shakespeare, *As You Like It* Act 3 Scene 4

# 1

# Connie and Max

Although I have only just begun to write about Maxwell in my Introduction, it is time to introduce my other subject: Annie Constance Smedley. Born in 1876, she was several years older than Maxwell.

Constance became an entrepreneur, illustrator and prolific writer, while Maxwell was a totally focused artist who also wrote about painting (and children's stories and other subjects such as America and Italy) and created stage designs and costumes. When they became a couple they were often spoken of as "Connie and Max" – a pair rather than as individuals. I shall call each of them by their abbreviated name, as others usually did. Together and separately they initiated, nourished, and developed arts projects across a wide range of activities including illustration, dancing, acting, embroidery and making stained glass.

With one important exception at the start of this book I follow the chronological sequences of their life events as far as possible. I describe their families, childhood, adolescence and achievements before they met, and then I write about them when they married, planned projects together and translated them into finished creations. Connie, after a life marred by illness and limited mobility, died in 1941,

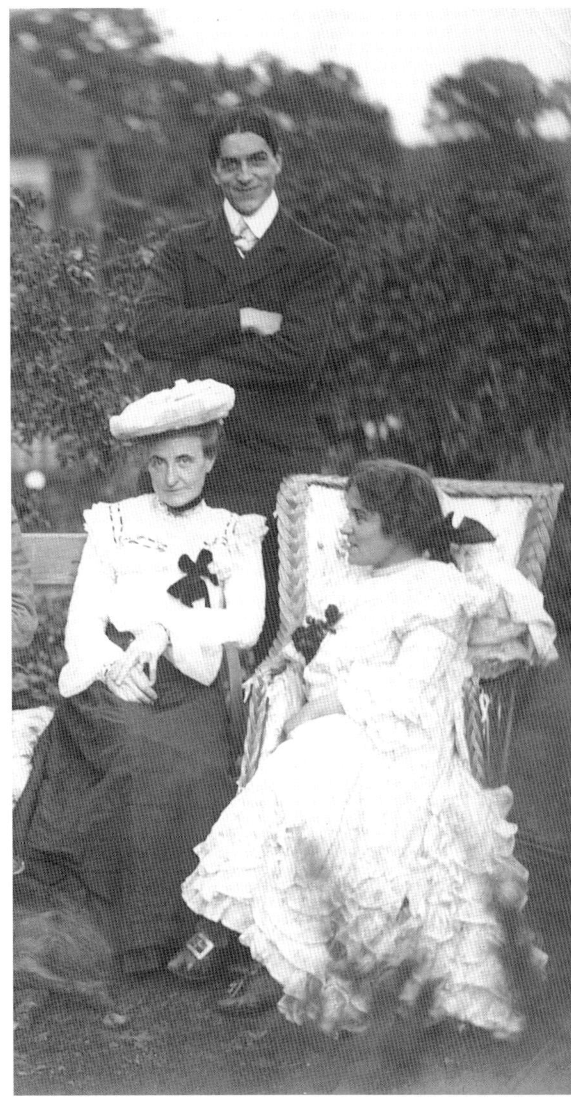

*Connie, with her mother and brother.*

but Max survived for another thirty years and died when he was ninety-two, in 1972. My father, born in 1905, was not of the same generation as Connie and Max, and I have therefore had to work him into the story where I can.

Despite my intention to keep to a straightforward timetable, I shall – as I mentioned above – begin with one particular episode in the couple's lives.

This event was *The Historical Pageant of Progress.* It took place when Connie was 35 and Max was 30 (at that time my father would have been about six years old and had no connection whatsoever with the pageant, nor with the Smedley or the Armfield families). The enterprise involved both Max and Connie and was a significant undertaking. A later chapter will put the pageant in its correct place in time, explain how it came into existence and quote newspaper reviews about it. Also, I shall discuss the issue of the contribution made by Connie and Max to the event.

But now, please accept the scene described below. It cannot be too far from the truth.

# Pageant

Imagine a couple walking along a field path in the Cotswolds on a perfect summer afternoon. On the afternoon of Thursday 7th September 1911, to be precise. Imagine what the woman and man might have said and done and seen on their stroll to Stroud from a village such as Minchinhampton or Slad, or Cashes Green, just a couple of miles away.

They would have welcomed the distant dark green hills, the exercise, the promise and purpose of the outing. They would soon have seen others heading in the same direction, and still more walkers would have joined them where a stile had to be climbed or a stream crossed. Little knots of people might have paused from time to time to gaze at the view and point out places they knew, such as the river Frome at Damsons Bridge or the mill chimneys. Excited children would have been running up to the head of the group, then dropping back, then taking off again. The walkers would have nodded greetings to the families and neighbours from various villages, and enjoyed the wild flowers, the sun and the loud skylarks singing above them.

When a lad shouted and waved a stick above his head, a cheer went up, and the walkers suddenly realised that they had become part of a loose procession. Then, when they saw Stroud spread out in front of them, most people stood still for a minute or two. Ahead was Rodborough Fort, the steeple of St Laurence and their destination: Fromehall Park Football Ground, without its goalposts.

Laughter and conversation grew as the people reached the road leading into Stroud and met up with others who had started from different places. Some pulled and pushed carts loaded with unusual cargoes: home-made armour and weapons, blankets, planks of wood, poles, clothes, rope, chairs and even babies. Most people were on foot, but many were on horseback, on bicycles, in motorcars and vans.

Looking further afield, the couple would have noticed that while in some fields there were stooks waiting to be collected, in others the uncut hay was swaying into wind-driven patterns. The absence of workers was no surprise, for the event they were heading for at the Football Ground promised – at least for three days – to be even more important than getting the harvest in.

And now strong smells of horse dung reached them, and then they found themselves in the midst of a flock of sheep clattering along the road. A shepherd and his dog led the baaing Cotswolds across and off the bridge, through a five-barred gate and into a field.

As the couple reached the ground where the pageant was to be held, they made their way to the ticket desk. They decided on seats at two shillings and sixpence, and set off at once to find good places. There were nearly two hours to go, but even so they had to push their way through to the front of the crowd.

There was so much to look at. A wide open space, the stage, stretched ahead and to their left and right. The most expensive rows of seats were filling up, while other members of the audience made themselves comfortable on the grass, or on rugs. A few actors already in costume – a Druid here, a soldier there, three children carrying leafy branches – were hurrying away to the far side of the stage. It looked as if some props – a step ladder, bundles of clothes, a bucketful of potatoes – were being delivered to a doorway where a flag waved. Some of the spectators were reading the Programme while others beckoned their friends to sit next to them, and still others tried to work out where the music was coming from. The couple whose route was described now claimed their places, and were wondering how many would assemble for this performance of *The Historical Pageant of Progress*. They had heard it would surely be hundreds, but that couldn't be right, could it?

An hour or so later three sudden blasts of a shrill whistle pierced the noise of talking, baaing and neighing and caused the audience to take their seats, cease chattering and gradually fall silent. After a further expectant five minutes an upright noblewoman in an ornate white dress rode into the centre of the stage on a gleaming black horse. Both rider and mount looked magnificent.

This noblewoman was *The Spirit of Progress*, and it was she who started the pageant. She spoke in a clear voice:

> *"Friends, you are welcome. Here in many a guise,*
> *'Tis our intent to set before your eyes*
> *From ancient records and from local tales*
> *The story of these Cotswold hills and vales,*
> *And from our living pictures you shall see*
> *The march of progress and of liberty."*

So, the pageant had begun, but how was it that such an enterprise was embarked upon, and what did it signify or represent?

To answer that we need to look at the people who were most concerned with it. The names most often associated with the pageant included Max and Connie, but who, exactly, were they and how did they come to be there?

3

# Connie's Early Life and Family

Connie was born in Handsworth, Birmingham. William T. Smedley, her father, born in 1851, studied to become a chartered accountant and established his own successful firm of accountants. His financial fortunes were not consistent but he became very well off over his lifetime. He was curious about people and the world and it seems that he was a driven man who, once on the track of a new idea or scheme – and he had several of these – pursued it with energy and diligence. He was also extremely generous and gave money to a range of causes, including a special one that we shall come to later.

William and his wife Annie Elizabeth Duckworth married in 1875. They were both 23. Annie Constance was their first child. She was followed by another girl, Ida (born in 1877) who was usually known as Di. Then there was a boy, William (born in 1883), known as Billie.

Connie's father was an unusual man. As well as running his own business, he became a key director, when only in his twenties, of a charitable organisation entitled The Birmingham Hospital Saturday Fund. In the 1870s there were concerns about the County Lunatic Asylum. It was also recognised that good medical care was needed but was not freely available to people convalescing. The BHSF came into being to raise money to pay for new buildings, renovations, staff and equipment, and William Smedley donated a substantial amount to it over a period of years.

The home created by his generosity, Tyn-y-Coed, was available to men who lived or were employed within a radius of five miles of Birmingham Town Hall. Preference was given to applicants who regularly subscribed to the Fund.

The place was an instant success. Patients and their employers often expressed appreciation of this great boon for Birmingham. Sick workers recovered and returned to work much sooner after a stay at Tyn-y-Coed and many of the men made new friendships and developed a deep sense of comradeship.

But William Smedley, atypically for such a young man, wanted to do still more. In particular he wanted to increase the provision of medical aid and establish a nursing home. He provided the vision, initiative and (again at least partly from his own pocket) the means to get things under way.

Though Birmingham was the business centre of the BHSF William Smedley made a point of visiting the Tyn-y-Coed convalescent establishment when he could. This meant 100 mile-long journeys to and fro between Birmingham and Llanrhos, a tiny community situated on a small bump of land on the north coast of north Wales. Later his wife and family – including Connie, of course – would accompany him and enjoy peaceful, rural breaks from the city.

But William Smedley's successful career as an accountant was overtaken by his other interests. He re-invented himself as a successful businessman in the nascent developments in film at that time. He also accepted the chairmanship of the company which was developing Roneo copiers, and, most importantly, he was for three decades the chairman of the British Mutoscope and Biograph Trust Ltd., the largest British film company in the Victorian period. Furthermore he was involved with Kinora, the business which invented home movies.

A history of Roneo, published by Roneo-Vickers in 1978, gives an idea of the man and some of his other interests:

*"In the office he showed a severe but paternal attitude towards staff and he could at times become exceedingly irate, when his large walrus moustache had a warning habit of bristling forward. He was a knowledgeable expert on roses, being a prominent member of the National Rose Society, with some 10,000 plants in his grounds. His other absorption was his extensive and valuable library of Elizabethan and Jacobean literature, his study of which led him to the conviction, which he claimed to be able to prove, that Bacon was the real author of Shakespeare's works. He was a keen photographer and astronomer."*

Connie must have been well aware of her father's passion for antique books even if she did not share it, and in the same way she must have known at least something about his work with the British Mutoscope and Biograph Co. After all, he was at the cutting edge of something new and brimming with tremendous potential: moving pictures.

British Biograph became the first company in the world to produce film. In September 1899 it filmed extracts from Shakespeare's *King John*. It was important enough for Herbert Beerbohm Tree (probably the most popular actor-manager at the time and who, in 1904, founded the Royal Academy of Dramatic Art) to be the director and also play the title role.

Four one-minute scenes were made at British Mutoscope and Biograph's special revolving film studio on the Embankment in London; and in a co-ordinated international promotion the scenes were shown at theatres throughout

Europe on the opening night of the live performance, rather as live streaming is done today.

By about 1905 William was an extremely rich man, but after WW1 his fortune declined. However, in 1912 he published his book *The Mystery of Francis Bacon*, an academic literary work. As a result of Connie's intervention (when in her thirties) William corresponded with John Howell, an antiquarian bookseller in the US. He reluctantly sent that book, and others, to the US:

*"I am so utterly ashamed of the treatment that English literary men have extended to Bacon that I should be glad to see my books go to America and know that the most suitable memorial was to be found there. I am afraid this is unpatriotic but the English deserve to lose every pleasure connected with the author of the Shakespeare plays and the translation of the Bible, or rather the authorized version in the early editions of which I am rich."*

The books eventually went to the Folger Library in New York.

Another typical event initiated by William Smedley was a dinner "to propose the memory of Francis Bacon", held at the Limpley Stoke Hydro Hotel (near Bath) on Thursday, the 22nd of January, 1931. It was the 370th anniversary of the birth of Bacon, though that fact would perhaps not have been known by many of the guests unless they had read their dinner invitations carefully.

All in all, it is obvious that Connie's father was a man who managed to fit a lot into his life. He did nothing by halves, and it seems highly likely that Connie's own energy and drive was influenced by his lifestyle. He died in 1934.

Annie, Connie's mother, came from a different background to that of her husband. Her father had been a coffee merchant but she had wide interests, was active in several charitable fields, such as (rather surprisingly, perhaps) running classes for young men who could not read. She had lived in France and spoke fluent French, and had won an award from the French authorities for contributing to an Anglo-French project. As Connie and her siblings grew up Annie proved to be as strong and as practical a mother as William was a father.

This positive attention from both parents who, between them, were well able to provide what the family needed, was especially important for Connie – as opposed to her sister and brother – because when she was three or four years old it became clear that she had a disability which resulted in her not being able to walk without sticks or (later, when an adult) crutches. The cause of this was usually attributed to one of two things. In *Crusaders,* Connie's reminiscences, she writes that she was "dropped by a nurse" when she was an infant. Other people, however, think it more likely that she was unfortunate enough to have contracted the polio virus sometime within the first few years of her life. Her lack of mobility became more evident as she grew, and her noticeable different posture and height meant that she could not participate at all in some activities, while in others, such as playing the violin, she reached the same standards as did her sister. It was also the case that Connie, like many who had polio (if that is what it was), experienced ill health through much of her life. Things became worse as she got older, for not only did her condition deteriorate so that she needed a wheelchair, but she became almost blind with cataracts.

What impact might her disability have had on her parents? Each of them was only 23 when she was born and they had only married in 1875, the previous year. They are unlikely to have known much about how to look after her and they probably had no experience of caring for someone who needed a good deal of practical and emotional attention and support. We can presume that the Smedleys were looking forward to their first child with excitement and some anxiety, as do all loving parents, but there was nothing to suggest that there was anything amiss with the pregnancy, birth or baby. It seems that Connie might have been several years old before it became impossible to ignore that things were not as they should be and that her condition was as likely to worsen as to improve. William and Annie must have sought medical advice but may have been unable to contradict rumours about the reason for Connie's disability, wrongly attributing the ill person's condition to another cause: an unhygienic home where disease festered.

The polio vaccine was decades away in the future – it was developed in 1956 and came into use a year later. During the late 1800s some of the treatment was experimental and the result of guesswork. We have no record of what happened to Connie, nor the extent of her paralysis, but most patients like her would have been subjected to at least one "treatment" such as being put in a plaster cast, or in an iron lung, or in water. Other methods included electric shocks and injections and the application of poultices. Worst of all, it seems that some patients were just left to lie in hospital for months.

A census states that the Smedleys employed a nurse, and as Connie grew the nurse must, presumably, have been responsible for helping her learn to balance and walk.

William and Annie seemed to cope well with Connie's disability, and while we cannot know what they thought and felt about the situation, and what choice, if any, they had over any future pregnancies, they went on to have another two children. First came their daughter Di, just one year after Connie was born. It must have been a huge relief for the Smedleys that there were no health problems

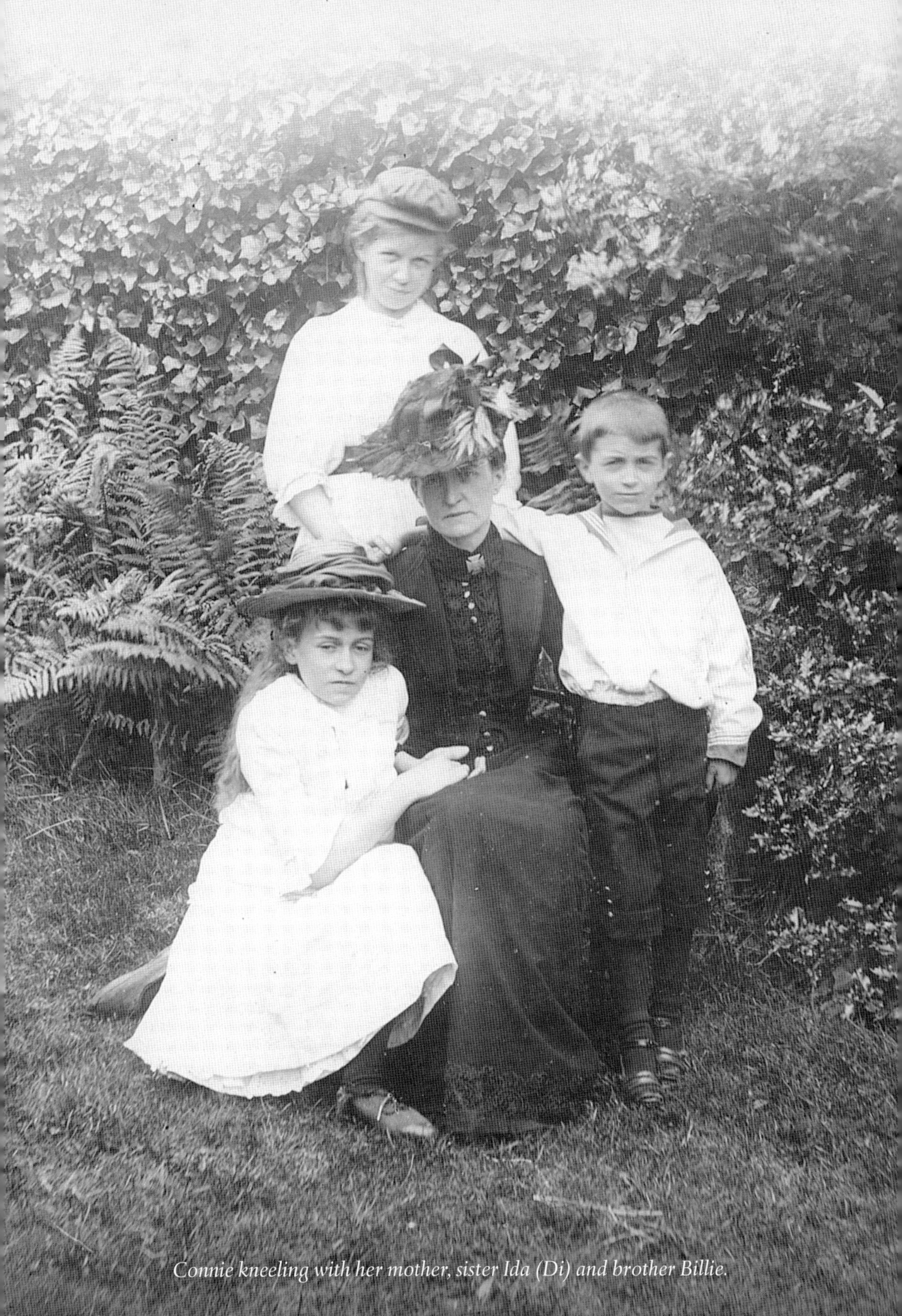

*Connie kneeling with her mother, sister Ida (Di) and brother Billie.*

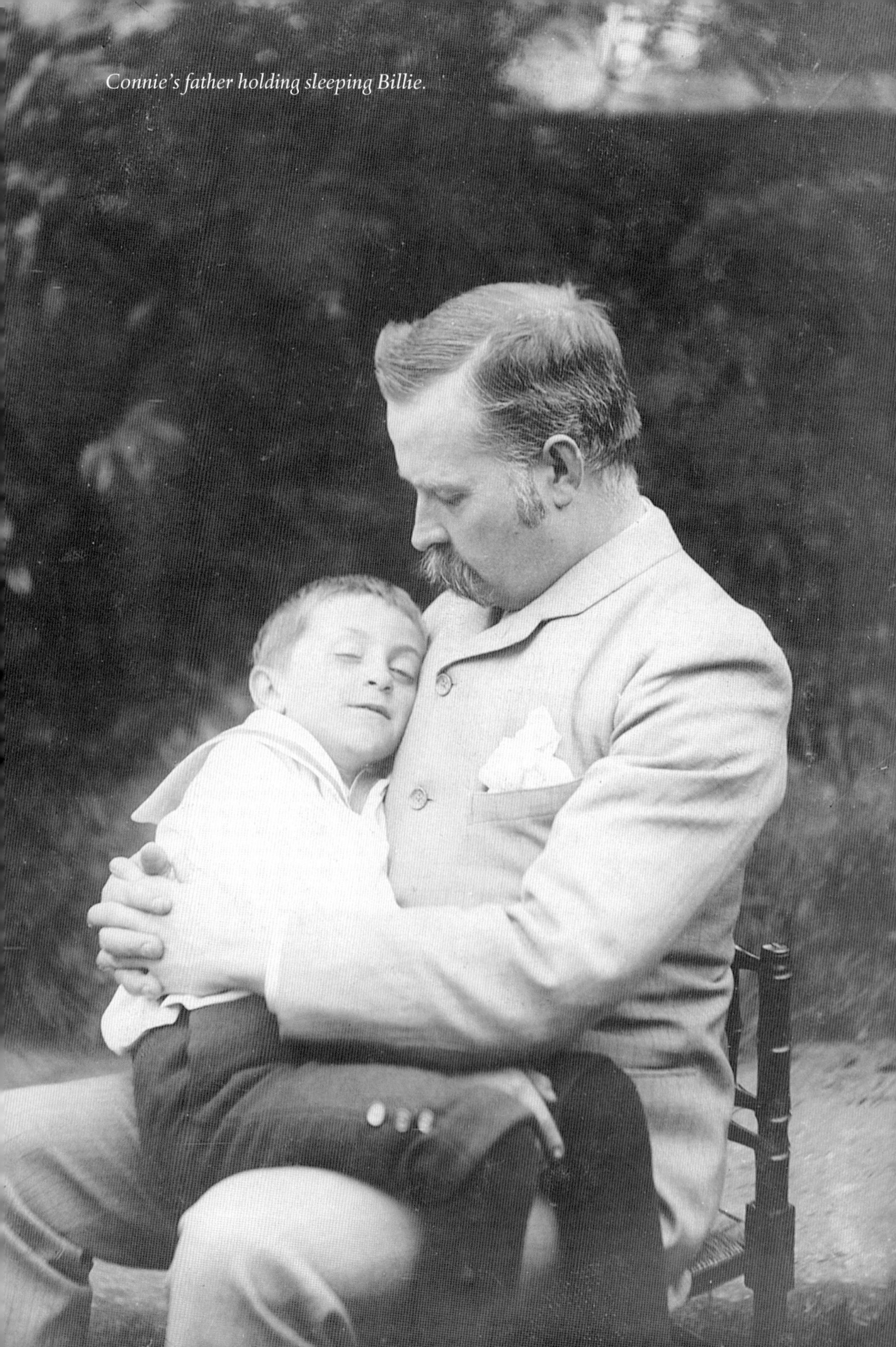

*Connie's father holding sleeping Billie.*

at or after the births of Di and their third child Billie. It seems that Connie was full of energy despite her condition, and all three children enjoyed a lively childhood.

The Smedley family moved house an unusual amount of times. Constance would have called many of her addresses "home" even if she was only in residence there for a short while. It may be the case that the Smedleys rented at least some of these houses rather than owned them, but whether that was so or not, each move must have been quite an upheaval. Perhaps this is why Connie hardly blinked when, as an adult, she was on a number of occasions at least partly responsible for supervising packing and rearranging rooms and furniture and organising re-decoration when the family moved.

In 1904 the Smedleys moved between houses in Birmingham (Sefton Villas, Birchfield Road and Ashley Gardens) to houses in London. As Connie, Di and Billie grew up they lived variously in Russell Square, Mecklenburgh Square and Chelsea. But they still retained, for holiday purposes, the house they owned in Llanrhos, another in Sheepcote near Maidenhead, and later even others, as at Bourne End. A final move was, in 1925, to a house in Limpley Stoke (in whose hotel William would hold his dinner to celebrate Bacon).

All the Smedley households would have been comfortable, attractive and spacious, and there must in most of them have been several staff with domestic and outdoor duties.

4

# David's Beginning

*October 12th 1905*

Annie Williamson gazed out of the door and across the mine. The baby was asleep in her arms. The scene in front of her was sparse and dry, and it always struck her as curious that something as beautiful as gold could not be got out of the earth without machinery and mess.

She turned her wedding ring round her finger. She and William had been married now for over four years: four very happy years. What would her life have been like if she had stayed in Greenock? She'd have had none of the adventures she had had. She would probably have stayed in Scotland and gone no further than Edinburgh.

As she reached down to pick up a toy car for James, she reflected on William. He also came from Scotland, but he had already been all over the place: Italy, Mexico and now Australia. He was the metallurgist here in Canbelego. She had not met anyone who had travelled and studied so much. She was proud of William who knew about so many things: stampers, poppet heads, cyanide plant and water condensing plants. He had explained about lodes and ores, which for some reason made gold sound heavy.

But what was of most importance to the couple now was David, this darling second baby. She looked across towards the mine just as he was beginning to make little waking-up noises.

While some of the buildings in her line of vision were substantial wooden constructions, others were mere shacks. Looking left, she could see the slime pit and the Raff wheel. To her right her view stretched towards Hidden Treasure and Budgery mines, and the low slopes beyond. Thank God she and her precious little family were living comfortably. Indeed, thanks to William's skills, they were more than comfortable.

She looked past the red water tank and noted how the evening light played on the trees. When she had a chance she would try to paint the scene. Since having the baby she seemed to have had no time to paint. Now, stepping round James who was pushing his car up against a fold in the rug, she reached across to her

12

book of watercolours and opened it with her left hand. Inside the thick, black cover she had written, with pride and pleasure:

*Annie SR Williamson, Mt Boppy NSW.*
*54 Union Street, Greenock.*

She began to turn the pages. Most of the pictures were of trees and big ponds or lakes. She had signed each one, and on the back of each she had written the name of the place she had painted: Inland Bay, Cronulla, NSW; Wymera tank beside hut.

All in all she was pleased with her painting efforts and looked forward to doing more. David gave a tiny shudder, and Annie looked down at him again. What a treasure.

This place was home. Of course it was nothing like her real home in Greenock, but she had come to like it, and it was where she would be living for at least some years.

Union Street seemed a long way away, and so did her two middle initials for names that were never used here in Australia: S for Stark and R for Ridpath. While James was happily climbing on and off a big cushion she pulled David to her and sang him a few bars of *O Can Ye Sew Cushions*:

*O Can Ye Sew Cushions? And can ye sew sheets?*
*And can ye sing ballooloo when the bairn greets?*

*And hee and haw birdie, and hee and haw lamb;*
*And hee and haw, birdie, my bonnie wee lamb!*

Annie longed to show her children to her mother, but knew that that would not happen for many years. She would have to wait until they were older, and then she would take them to Scotland.

But who knew what might happen before then? Sometimes she feared that she would never see her parents and her home again. She settled David against her breast and helped him latch on. Once he was settled and sucking she lent back and shut her eyes.

Yes. Things were good.

5

# Max's Childhood and Youth, and Quakerism

But what of Maxwell Ashby Armfield, the other subject of this biography? He was born on October 10th 1881 into a well-off Quaker family in Ringwood, a small town situated in the New Forest in Hampshire in the south of England. At the time of Max's birth its population was about ten or twelve thousand.

Joseph J. Armfield, Max's father, would have been known to everyone because he was the founder and head of the Armfield Iron Works, a very profitable and expanding engineering business employing plenty of local labourers and iron workers. He had served his apprenticeship at Carshalton in Surrey and moved to Ringwood in 1875 with the aim of making better quality agricultural machinery. He knew the local miller, Mr Munden, who was already established in the same business with waggon wheels and farmyard machinery, and making and repairing millstones. As well as being a miller Mr Munden was described as an engineer and iron and brass founder and it was he who had established the ironworks in Christchurch Street, in premises which had formerly been a brewery. Joseph Armfield was impressed by what Mr Munden had achieved and was achieving, and within a matter of months, he had bought his entire business and taken over sole control, using the business name of Munden and Armfield and Co. This enterprise thrived. Joseph had not only ambition, sound business sense and excellent technical knowledge, but he shared his natural warm nature with his employees, colleagues and customers. It was said of him, *"His normal working day was from 6 am till well after midnight. Every one of his men regarded him as a personal friend, and there were few working mornings when he was not in the shops before breakfast, cheerily greeting the men as he supervised the work in hand."*

In 1876 he employed 30 men. In the 1880s he built more mill machinery, and installed it widely in England. By then the Armfield name was known and respected in its field. In 1890 the name Munden was dropped and a new frontage designed to impress customers was made out of cast iron. Joseph went on to design water turbines, and he showed his first roller mill at the 1881 Exhibition, when he was not yet thirty years old. He gained a first prize at the Centennial Exhibition in Melbourne in 1888, and in 1889, another medal at Birmingham. The business expanded and peak production was reached in 1915.

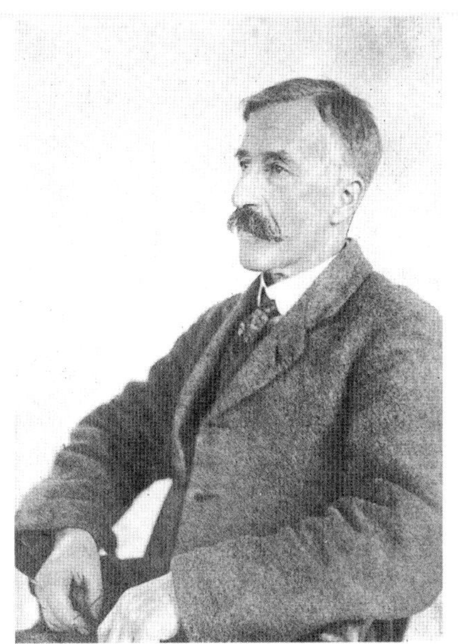

# Joseph John Armfield – Hampshire Quaker Ironmaster

### by D. A. E. CROSS

*Whose illustrated history of Ringwood industry was recently published: copies may be obtained from the author (2s. 6d.) at Moonrakers, Ducklington Lane, Witney, Oxon.*

ABOUT 1835 the last gallons of the once-famous Ringwood ale were brewed in the vats of the brewery of Stephen Tunks in Christchurch Road, Ringwood. Tunks, also the owner of a bank in the town, had suffered rather heavy financial losses, and both his bank and brewery closed down, though ale continued to be brewed at Carter's brewery in Bridge Street. Part of the brewery buildings were sold to William Munden, a blacksmith, and Munden, an enterprising craftsman, soon built up a flourishing little business, repairing waggon wheels and farm machinery, making and repairing millstones and milling machinery, even manufacturing patent textile machinery for the cloth weavers of Thompson and Westlake at East Mills, Fordingbridge. In 1859 Munden was described as " a miller, engineer, iron and brass founder," and it is from these early beginnings that the presence of almost all the large engineering firms now in Ringwood can be traced.

In 1875 another personality appeared on the scene, and it was he more than anyone else who was to mould the development of Ringwood's major industries. Joseph John Armfield, a young man of 23, visited Ringwood that summer and at once fell in love with the sleepy little New Forest town on the banks of the beautiful Avon. He visited Munden's little foundry and workshops, and was so taken with the possibilities of the business that the following year, 1876, he entered into partnership with William Munden and then, within a few months, bought the entire business and took over sole control. J. J. Armfield had been born in Jewin Crescent, London, of Quaker parents, and he had been brought up in the Society of Friends, being educated at a Friends' school. Always interested in science and engineering, he had served a strenuous apprenticeship to engineering at John Smith's at Carshalton, Surrey, and brought all his enthusiasm to the Ringwood workshops.

The business was run as " Munden, Armfield & Co." for several years after 1876, William Munden's name appearing in the accounts even up to 1880. The enterprise soon grew and prospered, gaining more than a local reputation, and this was largely due to the personality of J. J. Armfield himself. " His normal working day was then from 6 a.m. till well after midnight. Every one of his men regarded him as a personal friend, and there were few working mornings when he was not in the shops before breakfast, cheerily greeting the men as he supervised the work in hand . . ."

The Stuckton Iron Works, near Fordingbridge, has been in existence since about 1770 as an iron foundry and farm machinery works. In 1870 it was being run by George Shepherd, son of Mrs. Maria Shepherd, who had inherited the family business about 1810. At Stuckton a Cornish engine provided power for the works, forge and pattern shop. It is said that the first portable steam engine was built at Stuckton in the early 19th century. Shepherd sold the Stuckton works to J. J. Armfield in 1872, thus providing the Ringwood firm with a larger and well-equipped foundry.

In the 1880's Armfield built and installed much mill machinery in mills along the Avon Valley and elsewhere in England and Wales, for the firm was now getting nationally known. Roller-mill plants were being introduced into the milling industry, and



*Newspaper article about Joseph Armfield.*

Changes over the years mean that it is impossible to ascertain exactly where Joseph Armfield's family lived, but his home and workplaces were clearly very close to one another. Both Christchurch Street and the nearby Christchurch Road would have been busy and noisy with horses and carts, heavy boots, the clang of tools and the transportation of incoming metal and outgoing industrial plant.

Max's parents went on to have two more children. Three years after Max came Margaret, known as Daisy, and then, five years later, Joseph Harold, known usually as Harold, was born.

There is little written about Max when he was a child but in the notes he wrote in his autobiographical journal he remembered how he used to feel when preparing for a holiday:

*"My sailor suit was made of blue and white striped cotton with the usual deep-blue braided collar and well I remember the exaltation the sight of it always gave me, for it was worn only on such red-letter days as expeditions seawards whereas my sister's secure white sunbonnet that made her look just like a minute Quakeress, was an everyday affair."*

The Armfields often went to Porth Gwarra or Sennen where people used horse-drawn bathing-machines to get into the sea. But apparently Max was contemptuous of such things and always bathed from behind rocks or from a home-made tent. He loved the sea, the rocks and the sky, especially when the family had the place to themselves.

Simplicity of dress was important to Quakers. Two hundred years previously William Penn, one of the most influential Quakers, had given this advice:

*"Chuse thy Cloaths by thine own eye, not another's. The more simple and plain they are, the better. Neither unshapely, nor fantastical; and for Use and Decency and not for Pride."*

Max's mother, like his father, was also a Quaker although she had grown up as a Baptist, but while some sources state that she came from the west of England, in Penzance, Cornwall, others believe she came from Scotland.

Quakerism, also known as the Society of Friends, began in the 1650s. Its roots were in Christianity, and its founder was the dissenter George Fox (1624-1691) who was the son of a weaver. William Penn, who was expelled from university and not allowed to complete his degree because he criticised the established church, became a Quaker and then went on to found the state of Pennsylvania in America.

Typically, Quakers, and anyone else who wishes to attend a Meeting for Worship, join together in a Meeting House for an hour each Sunday. There are no ministers, no services, no religious images, and no communal prayer nor hymns. The meeting is based on silence. In silence, people pray or think their own thoughts, but if someone decides they would like to share what they are thinking about or feeling, they can stand up and speak. This way of conducting a meeting has hardly changed over several centuries. A crucial tenet for Friends is their belief that *"There is that of God in everyman."*

Quakers are admired by many for their courage and their work in difficult situations at home and abroad. Their strong belief in pacifism and consequent refusal to fight in both world wars led many of them having to attend tribunals where decisions were made regarding their reasons. Some people considered conscientious objectors to be cowards, but others respected them. Friends were and are renowned for their positive conduct and their contribution to humanity and justice whether in their ordinary lives, or in the public arena. One of the best known facts about them was their work to end slavery.

# 6

# David's Bereavement

*Mount Boppy, Canbelego*
*December 28th 1912*

Holding David's hand, Annie went to answer the door. She wasn't expecting anyone. So why were these important people coming to the house? Even the mine manager was there. So was the doctor. They looked serious. What was wrong? What? *What?*

The mine manager spoke quietly.

Annie froze.

When she turned to go inside the men hesitated and then followed her slowly.

It couldn't be true. William had always had good health. There had been nothing wrong with him. Annie bent down and put her arms round James who clung to her as she began to weep. Only a few hours ago she had waved William off to work, so there must be a mistake.

But there was no mistake.

She was told William had died from angina.

There had been no indication that anything was wrong at all. He had suddenly collapsed in the assayer's office. He was 39 years old.

Annie gasped for breath, felt her heart pounding.

The men were shocked, and felt increasingly awkward and sad as they stood in the Williamson's small, tidy sitting room, unable to do or say anything except listen to Annie's wails and watch the boys tug at her clothes. They stayed with her until two of Annie's women friends who had heard the news arrived to comfort her.

Just then David stubbed his bare toe on a step and gave a yell of pain which caused more crying. Annie was gulping for air. Surely all this was not true. How could it be?

# More About Connie

The Smedleys cared greatly about their children's development and, as the end of the century approached, gave them all the support and encouragement they could. They must have had real fears about Connie's future. What would happen when she was too heavy to be lifted easily? What about going up and down stairs? And what about later on, when she developed sexually? Surely Connie's condition would affect her chances of marriage? Of life? Of happiness? Surely having children was out of the question? It was all unknown, but at times the Smedleys must have found it hard to remain optimistic.

William and Annie treated their first-born as they treated Di and Billie: they included her and praised her. In short, they loved their children, and an example of this was the way they encouraged all three of them to participate in Annie's evening meetings. It is perhaps more accurate to call these occasions soirées. Annie invited intelligent and even renowned guests to the house every month for music, good conversation and discussions. These might be held in French or in German, or the guests might focus on a particular composer. From an early age Connie learned the violin, and Di the piano. On occasion they played duets and later Connie wrote *"We were our parents' companions"*. Everything suggests that Annie must have been a particularly popular hostess.

Most parents like the Smedleys would have sent their daughters to a local private school when they were five or six years old, but Annie undertook to teach them at home. This decision could have been made because of Connie's physical difficulties or for financial reasons but the base line seems to be that Annie deemed her own ability to teach (at least up to a certain level) to be equal to that of teachers in schools. She was right: with their mother's intelligent tuition Connie and Di flourished, quickly proving themselves able to cope with both artistic and academic subjects.

*8*

# The Unexpected

The outcome of seeking information, or playing detective – whichever a researcher or a biographer likes to call it – cannot be predicted. Visits can be arranged to libraries or museums, or to a particular architectural feature, and even after booking a meeting with an archivist, you don't know exactly what you will find. So, occasionally, after having arranged an interview with a specialist, or visited the house of the person you are researching, you might find yourself sitting on a stool in a station café having to admit that you have little more to show for the day than the receipt for your rail ticket, some photocopies and a few photos which you've already decided won't be good enough for your book.

But the opposite can happen too.

In the first weeks of my research for this book I was told that Maxwell Armfield's archive was kept by Tate Britain. I knew there was a mass of information – boxes full of files – which would require a good number of visits if I was to work my way through all of them. I hoped to find things like press reviews of his books, notebooks, photos of paintings and advertisements for exhibitions.

Having found the two paintings, the main question occupying me as I walked along the Embankment towards my first research visit was *"Might I find something else about my father here?"* But when the Armfield files were delivered to my desk my attention swooped back to Max. There was masses about him, and I saw at once that I would have to be very lucky indeed to find any reference to my father. Though Max had written loving words on the back of the paintings he had given to my father, perhaps their contact had been fleeting.

It was immediately clear both that the Armfield archive held plenty of useful information, and that I had made a good choice of subject, because the contents of the files were well worth reading. Max had made some brief notes during his first months at his school of art, and I got a sense of what things were like for him in terms of meeting new people, attending classes (or not), and of course painting. Disappointingly, there was nothing there about my father. Nevertheless, when booking myself into the Tate for my next session with his archive, I thought it worth mentioning to the archivist that there was a possibility that there could be some correspondence between Maxwell and my father David Blair Williamson.

20

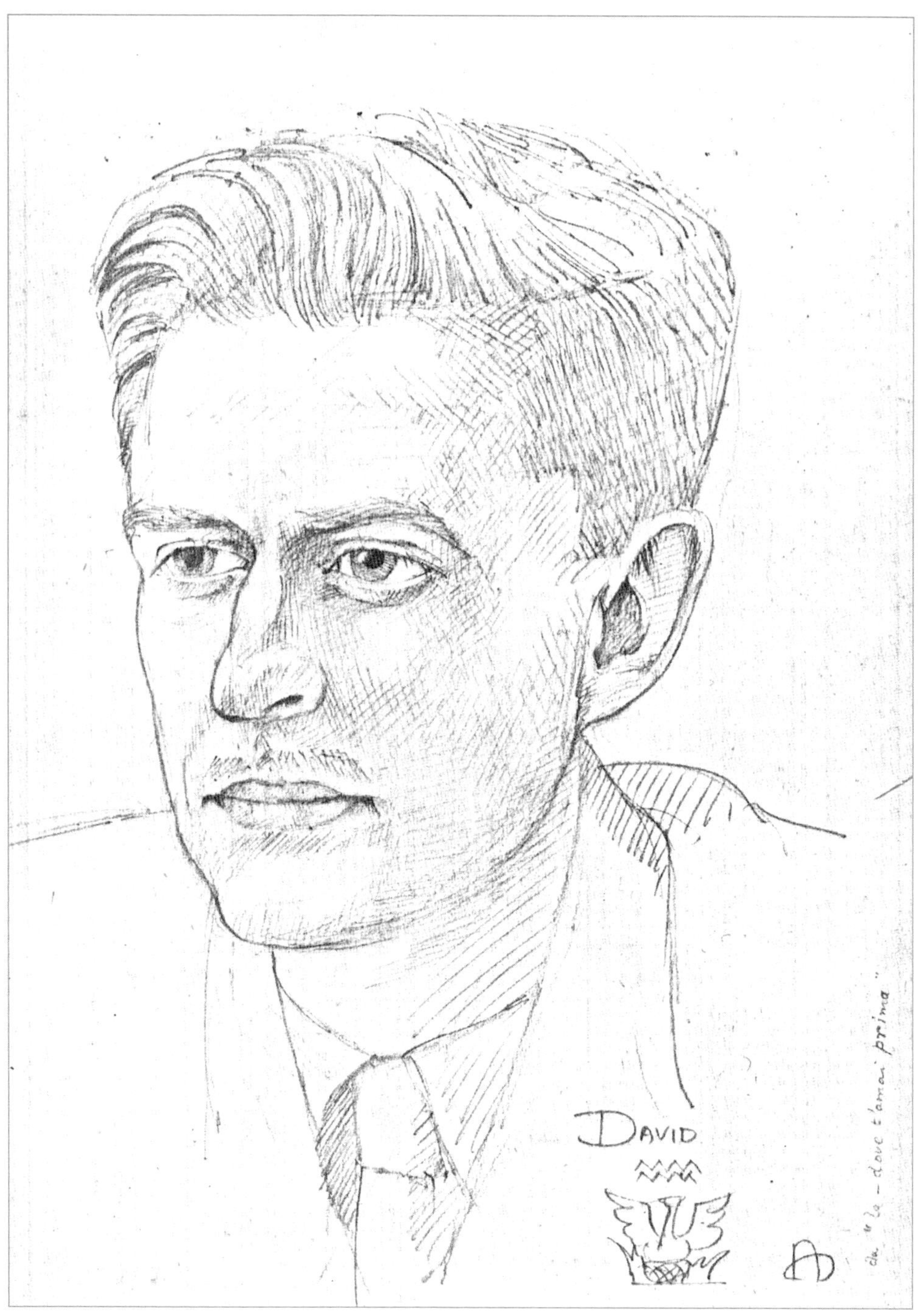


*Max's Sketch of David.*

And there was.

When I turned up for my second session at The Tate, there were three letters waiting for me. They were from my father to Maxwell, and had been found by one of the staff, together with a poem. The letters, obviously, gave me more information about David than about Max. David commented on Max's paintings, and on their friendship. So, quite separately from the biography I was hoping to write, I learned more about my father: his generous nature, his humour, his curiosity, his desire for all to be well for all people. I was five years old when he died, so most of what I knew about him had been related to me as I grew up.

I was immediately hungry to read these letters, so turned to them, temporarily abandoning the folders I'd reserved to study.

The letters, oddly addressed to "Michael" rather than to Maxwell,* were written on January 27th 1943, May 3rd 1943 and January 19th 1945. Written in my father's familiar and legible handwriting their contents were important because of their serious nature, their warmth and their reference to various organisations. In them my father expressed his opinion about the future of mankind, Max's paintings and literature they had both read.

David's letters mentioned my mother Phyllis and my older brothers only briefly. The letters did not make for casual or easy reading, but their mood, content and length indicated a strong companionship built on shared ideas.

Here are some quotes from the letter written on January 27th 1943 at my parents' house in Surrey (I am not sure when they bought this house). At that time, my father was 38, and Maxwell was 62. I would not be born for another six months or so:

*"I seem to have many letters of yours to reply to, but find it hard to 'step aside from the machine'** to do so!*

*Thank you for your Art in the New Order. I have read it through and as a first reaction would incline to the view that your explanation of our first meeting was indeed correct, but for the fact that thoughts such as are clearly in both our minds are equally clearly growing in many other minds today. To adapt Newton's simile I would regard us as two pebbles of similar colour or (complementary colours)*

---

*   I believe this alternative name was probably used because, when first they exchanged names, my father mis-heard Maxwell for Michael and the two decided that he should stick with it. Alternatively, it could have been one of the pseudonyms that Max used as he got older.

** By "machine" I understand my father to mean, "Busy and demanding daily life."

*washed together by the tide. However, be that as it may, I am delighted to find you saying in all your knowledge some of the things to which as you no doubt saw from my pamphlet have been feeling my way in the realisation that they are real and there and attainable."*

David's mention of his pamphlet is interesting. One has to be very keen on something before one gets down to writing a pamphlet about it. By definition, its content is brief and about something that matters to the writer but not given the importance it deserves. David wrote quite a few pamphlets.

The subjects raised in these letters were serious ones. One picture they corresponded about was Max's *Red Tape and Sealing Wax*.

My father wrote:

*"This stuck in my mind after seeing it and I meant to ask you … to explain its symbolism to me. It held my attention simply because I envied the free youth his joyous scissors and his clear happiness in liberation. I often feel the need of a pair of scissors like that and symbolically mankind could do with a liberator wielding a pair. But I am not sure that that is the thought in the picture."*

In the letter dated May 1943 Max thanked David for sending him *The Animal Book*, a children's book with illustrations by Max and text by Connie. It had first been published in 1922. David responded to Max:

*"They are original and colourful stories told with a fine sense of movement and life by linking with your illustrations – so that one wonders whether your wife wrote the stories for your pictures or vice versa."*

(In fact, it was Connie who wrote the text).

Almost exactly two years and, I believe, many letters (and possibly several meetings) later, David wrote to Max about a newly published book called *Dragon Beards versus Blueprints,* by a Chinese writer, Hsiao Ch'ien. I had never heard of it or its author. It is a slim volume with the subtitle *Meditation on Post-war Culture,* and is clearly literature for analytical and well-read intellectuals – people like Max and my father.

Best known as a sculptor, Hsiao Ch'ien included one illustration in his book. It is a highly detailed woodcut showing two men making some complicated machine.

Here is an extract from David's letter:

*"Cooperation in the world of tomorrow, as I see it, means blue prints today to ensure good environment for men, for children, but it will be a poor world tomorrow if dragons are obliged to live in chromium plated hygienic dens and to keep their beards trimmed to the statutory shape and length as laid down in Blueprint No. X 100955A."*

This letter also included comments from David about some of Max's paintings, and his hope to see more of his work as well as more of Max.

Clearly, Max and my father had a similar approach to the human condition – one which is hard to define, but characterised both by a serious attitude to the world and by a specific desire to contribute to positive post-war initiatives.

Unlike Max's essential equipment of paint and brushes, my father's tools were his typewriter, his pen and his voice.

I wondered how these two thoughtful men had met and guessed that they had been at some lecture or exhibition about one of the shared (minority) interests referred to in their letters. I was intrigued to realise that their friendship seemed to be very strong, and that their correspondence nourished them both. How often had they met? And how did David manage to squeeze anything extra into his already busy time?

And, a further unanswerable and crucial question, I wondered whether my mother had met Max, and what she thought of her husband writing letters to him late into the night? Had she too seen his paintings?

I think it likely that, while David (who, mostly for reasons of ill-health, did not have a steady job but was involved with various organisations) attended meetings and gave talks in different venues, Phyllis coped cheerfully with two small boys and a baby (me), and was ready to listen to David's activities when he came back to Walton-on-Thames in Surrey. My brother and I have numerous letters between Phyllis and David who experienced extremely difficult conditions exacerbated by war and post-war circumstances. They were both hugely optimistic human beings. Every single letter in both directions is full of love, warmth and good humour.

In one letter from his hospital ward, having told my mother about his inability to get enough sleep, David sent this quote from *Macbeth*:

*"Envoi*

*I am going to become one of those lads who study Shakespeare and deduce how he spent his life.*

*Sleep that knits up the ravell'd sleeve of care*
*The death of each day's life,*
*Sore labour's bath, balm to hurt minds*
*Chief nourisher in life's feast."*

My father added a note: *"Deduce from this that he spent a delightful weekend at Stratford Cottage Hospital."*

Max's situation was totally different to this. Importantly, Connie, (his wife whom he married in 1909 and whom we are gradually approaching), died in 1941 – only two years before David wrote the first of the letters I have mentioned. Max had therefore been a widower of several years when he was writing to and meeting David. He had never been close to his wife's family, but after Connie's death, he certainly saw Di and Billie from time to time, and he remained close to Daisy, his own younger sister.

# Max's Early Life and Schooldays at Sidcot

It is very likely that Max's mother was happy to conform to Penn's sartorial advice, for she led a very respectable life. The 1891 census states that the Armfield household in Ringwood included a governess and two servants. At that time the governess, Anne Macmillan, was nineteen years old and from Castle Cary, less than fifty miles away. It is possible that she was related to Douglas Macmillan (born 1884) of Castle Cary. He attended Sidcot, a Quaker School in Somerset where Max would be sent in 1890. Douglas Macmillan was appointed as head boy, perhaps a suitably responsible position for someone who, in 1930, would become the founder of the well-known charity, Macmillan Cancer Relief.

There were a number of Quakers in Ringwood, but their name is only remembered now in Quaker Court, presently accommodation for people needing support. One might have presumed that the Armfields would have attended the local Friends' Meeting each Sunday, and Diana Armfield (Max's niece who lived locally) said that the family would certainly have done so, and that Max's father Joseph would have been an elder (an older member who nourishes the welfare of the members of a meeting). But, strangely, there is evidence of only occasional attendance of the family at meeting. Indeed, in his journal Max refers to his childhood attendance at church and comments that going to a Friends Meeting or any church service when he was a schoolboy was an unusual event for him.

Max's parents encouraged their children to design, to paint and to make things and they took them to the National Gallery and the Royal Academy. These visits inspired Max, for later he wrote, *"I cannot remember when I was not drawing in some way."*

In his journal, the young Max recalled a change to his life:

*"One summer a certain Edmund Ashby, who was my mother's brother and a friend of my father came to stay nearby. He was the head of the Friends' school at Sidcot. I had never seen these cousins before and I quickly made friends with the youngsters.*

*There were obscene mutterings of 'school' which filled me with vague alarm and one fateful day I was informed that in the autumn I should see Howard (one of my new friends) for I was going away to the school where he lived."*

Howard, Max discovered, was one of the headmaster's children. And so, when he was eight and a half years old, Max was taken to Sidcot – a journey of some 70 miles.

Perhaps Joseph, his father, took Max, or perhaps he went with someone else, but either way, it must have been an adventure to leave home for this next stage of his life. The highly successful director of the prestigious engineering works would have been one of the first people in Ringwood to have a motor car, and to be taken to Sidcot by a mechanical vehicle would have been a note-worthy expedition both for its passengers and for those who saw and heard it. At that time, when cars were unreliable and expensive, many of the pupils would have arrived by horse-drawn vehicle, and some would have come by train.

Whatever method of transport Maxwell used, on his journey he would not have failed to notice differences in landscapes, villages, towns and the people he saw and met. It must have been quite an experience.

He might have been wearing his new school uniform:

*"(The boys) wore a shirt and tie, either with a suit or with a jacket and shorts. Sunday suits were navy, grey or charcoal but before the war the Lower School boys had to wear tight Eton suits – black jackets with a point at the back, black striped trousers, a white shirt front and enormous starched collars. The jackets were irreverently referred to as 'bum-starvers'. The boys also wore boaters, known as 'barges'."*

The day after arriving at Sidcot Max had to go to a Quaker meeting which he described later:

*"I had only been rarely to meeting before and I remember very well the horrid stuffy feeling I had the first morning after my arrival.*

*The youngest boys went in first and sat in front under the immediate shadow of the masters and overseers and awe inspiring people in the gallery. The perfect silence of so many people together was dreadful to me. I wanted to shout or do something. I had the same frightened sinking feeling of the stomach and in my chest that I always had in advance of a bathe before I could swim, and I wanted to swallow all the time only it made such a noise. I daren't for I was sure it could be heard over the Meeting House so I just sat frightened and almost faint with miserableness. It seemed years and years until the end man and the end woman shook hands and we filed out. How we hated it."*

Max had to attend meeting twice a week, and sometimes when he was there he tried to sleep, or make his mind go blank.

His thoughts would have included reflections on his daily life, his worries, his hopes, his family, the people sitting opposite, a small beetle making its way across the floor. Perhaps he prayed, and perhaps he listened to and benefitted from the spoken contributions made by Friends. But like most ten or eleven year old children in Quaker meetings, he would definitely have day dreamed for some of the time, and have been bored for many of the sixty long minutes (today, children usually only join the beginning or the end of the meeting, before or after their separate gathering). The Quaker Meeting for Worship lies at the heart of Quakerism, but in another diary entry he looked back:

*"I hate Sundays and always did: at school they made them the most dreary days of the week with two dismal meetings that were enough to send anyone against Friends."*

Gradually, Max would have come to know Sidcot's buildings, its routines, its members of staff and the other pupils. After several earlier educational ventures the school had been founded in 1808 with six boys and three girls. At the end of the 1890s there were 132 pupils – a small enough number for everyone to know each other, at least by sight. Edmund Ashby, Max's father's cousin, was headmaster throughout Max's time at the school, from 1892-1900.

Though not particularly keen on sport, Max probably played cricket with Howard and others. The boy's playground sloped which made things interesting on freezing winter nights when buckets of water were tipped down the slope in the hope of creating a good skid area of ice for the next morning.

Although the school was co-educational, there was, in fact, very little contact between boys and girls. Not many years before Max was a pupil, boys and girls had neither attended lessons nor socialised together. Conversations with the opposite sex – allowed only between brothers, sisters and cousins – were limited to an hour a day.

Max was one of a number of Armfields who went to Sidcot. The one who is mentioned most in this biography, other than Max, is Stuart. Born in 1916, he was a cousin of Max's, and his middle name was Maxwell. He studied Design and the History of Architecture before working as a set designer at Elstree. But, as a conscientious objector who declined to work on war propaganda films he was instead detailed to do agricultural work, which suited him very well. Later he decided to focus on his painting – especially Symbolism – and moved to

Cornwall in 1942, taking up painting full-time in 1945. His studio was in Looe and he had a strong connection with Polperro, living in several houses there over the years. He was on very good terms with Max. He died in 1999.

In Edmund Ashby's list of the advantages of co-education, he commented that all the pupils worshipped together, took meals in the same room, attended lectures together, shared picnics and joined in general games. He also said, *"Objections may be made on account of small flirts. I do not think that too much should be made of this difficulty. If carefully watched it is manageable."*

Max studied the usual school subjects, and the following direction, issued to teachers in 1921 – admittedly twenty years after Max and his cohort of pupils might have been subject to its impact – gives a flavour of the even more stringent standards required in earlier years. These are the Rules laid down as to the precise position to adopt while writing:

*"The scholar should sit with weight of body equally on both thighs – practically square to desk.*
*Both forearms should rest on desk not wrist.*
*Eyes should be at least twelve inches from paper.*
*The paper must lie practically square on desk and usually with the left hand edge opposite middle of body."*

In 1907 an inspection (the second one) of Sidcot was carried out by six members of His Majesty's Inspectorate. Though this report took place about eight years after Max left the school, it surely tells us something about Sidcot in Max's time. The report speaks highly of the then headmaster, Bevan K. Lean who was praised for being a man of marked organising capacity and educational zeal.

The inspection was thorough. One of the recommendations was that a fives court should be built. Another was that more baths were needed as there were only six for the whole school (boys and girls). But there was one comment which was expressed particularly vehemently: the inspectors pointed out that there was:

*"an astonishing inaccuracy of spelling throughout the school. This inaccuracy is quite phenomenal."*

It was suggested that all staff should address this appalling situation. Max must have been an exception, for there are no spelling errors in his work, though there may have been when he was a schoolboy. Or perhaps he was a beneficiary of the renewed attention to spelling?

The inspection covered every subject, and it seemed that art lessons were mechanical and prescriptive.

Were the inspectors interested in listening to the Sidcot School song being sung? It was probably not part of the inspection itself, but the inspectors might well have been astonished to hear it. It begins:

*"In the heart of the Mendips old Sidcot stands,*
*How her name like music thrills.*
*Long long may she rest like a white-robed queen*
*In the arms of these grand old hills."*

Nothing remarkable about the words, perhaps, but they were sung to the tune of the Marseillaise.

At Max's time at Sidcot the long-serving art teacher, Mr. Clark, had had no formal artistic training, and his lessons consisted of arranging geometric shapes which pupils were to draw in pencil. One schoolboy commented later, *"It was simply killing any interest in us"*. Only a select few were allowed to use paint.

In earlier years some children had enjoyed drawing, though there were better opportunities for those keen on sport, music and literature. However, a change of art teacher meant that things improved. The new loved and gifted teacher was likely to have been Theodore Compton, a committed Quaker who was an artist, illustrator, author and mountaineer. He lived locally and was a close friend of Sidcot, teaching art as and when necessary even though he was not a member of staff. Art gradually gained ground and the head even arranged for the staff to attend lectures on the teaching of drawing. These became part of the official curriculum and there were also voluntary classes.

Max gained something from the tuition available, but when he was about sixteen he became interested in posters. He worked hard on these in his study, in privacy.

Also relevant to Max's journey to becoming an artist are, in his auto-biographical journal, two important references to someone he called Uncle John. The first fact about John was that he could play *"Home Sweet Home"* on the violin without any notes at all (but what, exactly, was meant by this odd achievement?) and the other was that he painted pictures.

Max wrote:

*"I announced one day to my Mother my intention of being an artist when I grew*
*up – like Uncle John."*

*"But Uncle John isn't an artist, he's a solicitor."*
*"But he does paint pictures."*
*"Yes, sometimes, in his holidays."*
*"Well then he must be an artist."*
*"You can call him an artist if you like."*

The identity of "Uncle John" is not clear, but Max's resolution – made at the age of, perhaps, twelve or thirteen, could not be clearer.

The fact that Max stayed at Sidcot until 1897 (there are some slight discrepancies re dates) and that Joseph Harold, his much younger brother, was sent there in 1900 and stayed until 1908, suggests that Joseph and Margaret Armfield were very satisfied with the school despite it being so far from Ringwood. In addition, given that other family members had studied there (and more would do so in the future) they must have been not only very familiar with the school but actually fond of it. The boarding fees were £51 per annum, with ten shillings and sixpence extra for stationery and drawing materials, six shillings and sixpence for piano lessons, and nine pounds and sixpence for violin lessons.

But, for whatever reason, for his final school year Max was moved to Leighton Park, another Quaker boarding school (now co-educational but not so in Max's time). Although the reason for this move is unclear, it could have been simply because Leighton Park in Reading was more prestigious.

Most of the extant letters to Max when still a schoolboy were from his father. But this is one from his mother in 1984 written when he was 13. The letter is headed with Margaret's small sketch of a hill and some trees:

*"My dear Maxwell,*

*I suppose you have settled into regular school work again as we have made into our work at home feeling all the better for the change. I hope you have been enjoying your fruit and are not letting it get rotten, the pears will want looking at every day. I think about you giving up Latin, the more sorry I feel that you should drop it even for 3 months as a thorough knowledge of Latin will help you better to understand literature and appreciate what is best in it. So if you drop Latin now, ask if you will be able to continue it after Xmas. As you would not only be not getting on but going back, you would be sure to forget a good deal."*

*10*

# Connie Growing Up in Birmingham

At about the age of ten or twelve years, in around 1888, when Connie was able to get around with sticks, it is said that she was sent to King Edward VI School for Girls (in Birmingham), but the school (situated in Handsworth) was not founded until 1911 when it was formed from three schools. It is not known which of those three Connie and Di attended, but it was probably Aston, the one contributing most girls to King Edward's.

Connie was extremely active in mind and spirit during her school days, and one can picture her as being enthusiastic, confident and probably noisy. It is not hard to imagine her scooting along corridors, well-practised at finding the best way to negotiate stairs and doors, while talking and laughing with her friends. What she wanted was Life!

There were strict rules about behaviour, even when not on school premises: no talking to boys, no eating in the street, and a requirement to always wear gloves. Was this latter rule adhered to? Even in summer? It seems likely that Miss Nimmo, the orthodox and admired headmistress at that time, would have insisted on it.

Getting to and from school could be quite an adventure. While many girls came by bike, or walked (and a good number went home to lunch each day), others – including Connie – would have been driven there in a motor car unless they came by tram, train or even four-horse bus.

Despite the fact that Connie was both positive and prospering, not everyone considered her firmly established in the world. An indicator of how her life expectancy was regarded by some was when a relation writing her will made financial provision for various nephews and nieces, of whom Connie was one. It included a special clause which stipulated what should happen to Connie's share should she not reach the age of 21. Who knows how many other potential donors thought the same but did not voice it or act on it?

At school, Connie's natural inclination was to turn towards the arts, and to some as yet undefined activities that would interest or amuse people and put her in the public eye. She did not need to be actually on show, but she wanted to give her ideas room to breathe and to develop them, to achieve her aims and to gain

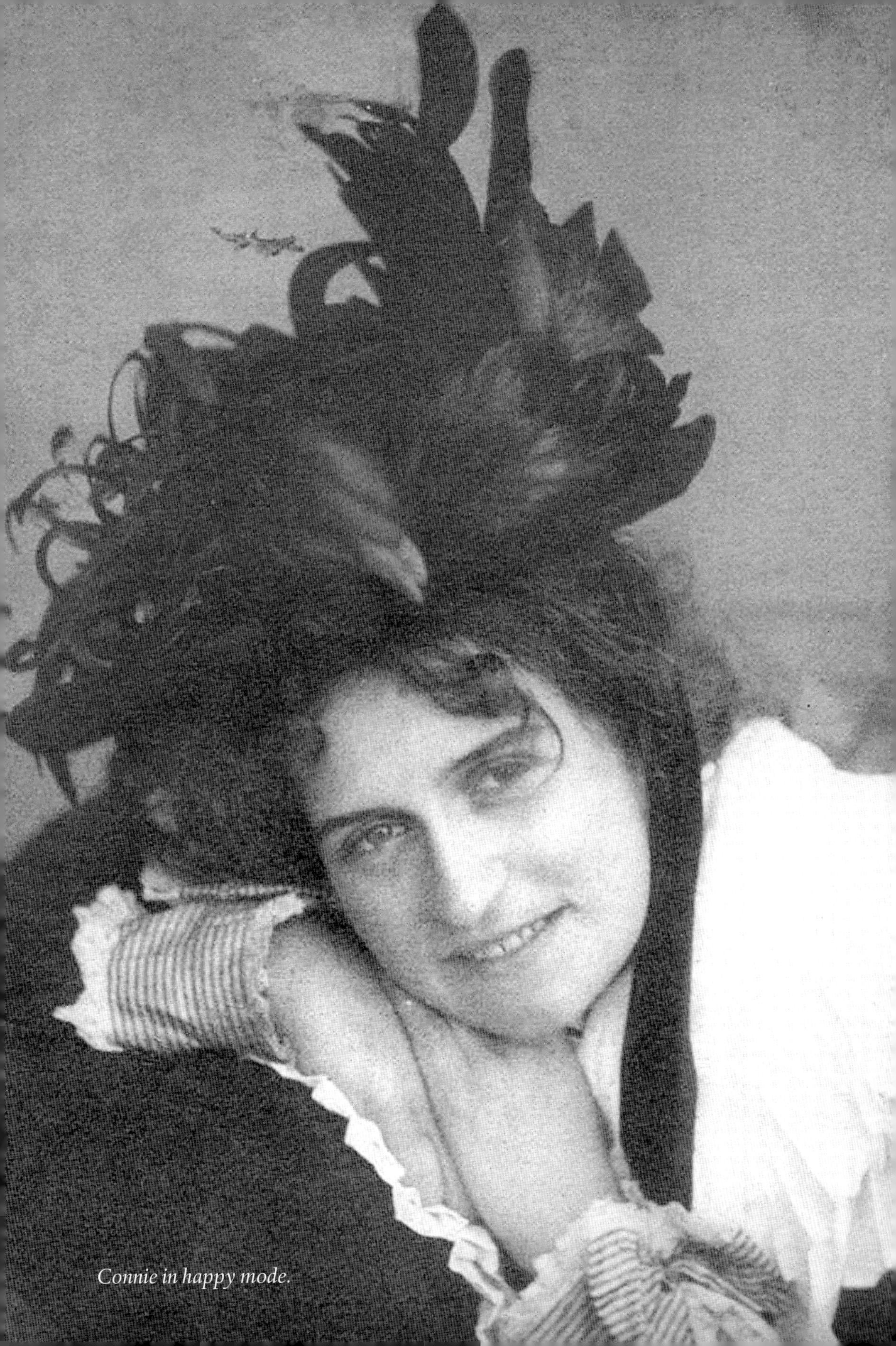

*Connie in happy mode.*

recognition at least, if not fame. At school she might well have been described loosely as "arty". Indeed, she probably would have been very happy to use that word to describe herself. Years later, when asked about success and failure, she said:

*"I've never thought about them, and certainly never about failure!"*

When Connie first went to King Edward's nature study was taught but science was not. However, as soon as science was on the curriculum Di turned towards it. By the age of about 13 both girls already knew clearly the direction they were heading in and what they themselves wanted to do.

In their own way, each of them was ambitious. An example of Connie's early focusing on activities which could, while she was at school, be broadly described as literary, was when she was curious about the meaning of one of Robert Browning's poems, and so wrote to the poet asking for clarification, which he supplied. This action was born of her initiative, curiosity and – on this occasion – desire to win a school competition. Browning's notes enabled her to perfect her entry, but she was so excited she failed to submit her essay by the cut-off time.

Undeterred, she was probably already embarking on other projects, such as a drawing she made and sent, when she was sixteen, to a London publication called *Pall Mall Magazine*. The editor not only accepted it, but paid her for it, thus cementing her growing interest in writing and drawing, beginning to make a name for herself and proving that initiative paid off.

We can imagine Connie rejoicing and proudly shouting her news to the world. Having tasted the buzz of success, she threw herself into not just writing stories and plays, but into getting those in authority to agree to let her take responsibility for dealing with all the permissions, properties and procedures they required. She achieved much of what she wanted, and she did so on her own personal merits without expecting to get special or empathetic treatment because she was disabled.

*11*

# Ida

Connie's sister Ida, known as Di, was a key member of the Smedley household, but one can imagine that life might have been difficult for her at times. Was it the case that Connie attracted an excess of attention because of her disability? Happily, there is no suggestion that there was any rivalry or resentment – sound evidence of their parents' care and support to both their daughters.

It was soon apparent to the school staff that Di would be a high achiever, for she was already winning her first awards and cups and generally showing her prowess – especially in science subjects.

Barbara Mclean (Di's daughter) describes an event from her mother's school days:

*"From the start chemistry was included in the timetable and she would have gained one hundred per cent marks in her first examination had her teacher not been Irish. As it was, marks were deducted because my mother referred throughout her answers to a 'chest chube'."*

Barbara also remembers a rhyme that her aunt Constance made up about her mother:

*"Now Con had a sister named Ida,*
*Who looked very paltry beside her.*
*For Di wasn't pretty*
*Nor clever nor witty*
*And so we won't stop to deride her."*

Not surprisingly, Barbara, when adult, felt for her mother when she heard this unkind (or amusing?) rhyme, but that's how siblings are sometimes. One cannot know what impact Di's academic achievements had on Connie who might have been jealous of them, or dismissive. What mattered greatly was that William and Annie must have been delighted that both of their daughters were thriving in their chosen fields of activity.

As Di approached the end of her time at school she was resolving to go to Oxford or Cambridge to study science. In the 1890s this was an unusual (and almost unachievable) course of action for a woman, but the school and William and Annie were absolutely behind her, encouraging her.

Over time the two sisters, initially very close – to the point of Di acting in Connie's plays – began to drift apart. While Connie increasingly focused on her rather unorthodox projects which Di had little time for, Di preferred to concentrate on her specialist career in science, so off she went to Newnham College, Cambridge, taking Warwick, her collie dog with her. She must have been disappointed when the authorities insisted he had to be boarded out.

This began at Cambridge University and progressed by her making one successful leap after another. She gained awards, took on new responsibilities, and moved into senior positions. Amongst her professional achievements were the following: becoming the first female Fellow of the London Chemical Society, winning a Beit Research fellowship and an Ellen Richardson Prize and publishing about forty scientific papers. Her particular subject area was fat metabolism and synthesis: words which would have meant little to Connie, and indeed, to many others.

This is an example of the sort of papers she wrote:

*"The Condensation of Aromatic Aldehydes with Pyruvic Acid."*

Di made her career in the Lister Institute of Preventative Medicine, where she met Hugh Maclean, the man who became her husband and with whom she had two children.

Di's grandmother had warned her that while her parents William and Annie were rightly proud of their daughters' abilities and achievements, Di must realise that, if she were to devote herself to them, *"she would be a social oddity, a bluestocking, and could never expect to marry or to have children."*

Before long she had made the decision not to focus down on pure medicine, as she had initially intended, but on biology and chemistry.

At university she liked both studying and making new friends. Some of these friends were men, and Di must have found ways of enjoying their company while somehow conforming with the rather unclear college instruction which stated that *"(the female) students could walk along with them* (presumably "them" means the male students?), *so long as they were going in the same direction."*

She moved to London in 1901 and worked there, and then back to Cambridge and Manchester University whcre she met Marie Stopes, the pioneering promoter of the birth control service designed to help women and men across the UK choose whether to have and when to have children.

Despite the hours she spent in laboratories, and on looking after her two children (who had been born despite grandmother's warning) and running a household, Di had the will, skill, time and energy to challenge the various barriers that most women faced every day.

She was an exceptional woman. The role she played in the Lister Institute was vitally important. Without fuss she proved to others – both men and women – that her work was every bit as well-executed as that of a man. In personal and political terms she was active in promoting women's issues to the point where she was a regular campaigner, encouraging others to participate and persuade. She can be counted amongst those leading suffragettes who wanted to replace resentment and rage with confidence and cooperation. She knew that this could not be achieved until women joined together. Di was a real example of the effort women have to expend and organise in order to cope with their work and their family responsibilities simultaneously, and often unassisted. Of course she was not advocating that women should shoulder all the problems of the world, rather that life's burdens and achievements should and could be shared.

While Di's desk was covered with notes and papers relating to meetings and minutes connected to the women's movement, Connie's was heaped up with papers of a different sort. Each of the sisters, in their individual way and by very different strategies, was working to improve the lot of women, especially their health and their overall well-being. In Di's case, her work was in the field of preventative medicine whereas Connie, though still only in her late teenage years, was networking with people in the arts world, and introducing others who she thought would be interested in her and interesting to know. Despite her youth she was beginning to foster relationships with those who most valued art, music, literature, drama and dance. These were not frivolous friendships, but ones which Connie learned from and contributed to. All these were to underline and extend her activities when she was a little older.

# Max Moves to Birmingham

Max and Connie both spent three years at Birmingham School of Art, although they knew nothing of each other until after they had left it. The two of them "missed" each other by a mere few months because Connie left the School in the summer of 1899, and Max did not join it until that autumn. Each of them changed their accommodation, too. Between 1899 and 1901 Constance lived in Sir Harry's Road in Edgbaston, while Maxwell's home was at 13 Wheeleys Road. These addresses are less than half a mile apart, but despite this proximity of date and place, one cannot know for certain when the pair met for the first time, but it was probably not until 1907.

The first entry of Max's diary, on Sept 14th 1901, starts with a neatly written Foreword. It speaks for itself:

> *"As this diary will be written firstly to amuse myself and secondly to instruct a possible future biographer I shall just put down anything that I think interesting and from that point of view shall make no apology to him for being egotistical in endeavouring only to be more or less accurate and as lucid as may be."*

So, Maxwell, at around twenty years of age, was already thinking – or even assuming – that in the future he will be the subject of a biography. He also, unsurprisingly, made the assumption that that biography will be written by a man. This intention, together with his assertion that his prime purpose in keeping a diary is to amuse himself, is happy evidence of his ambition and confidence. He believes he is already on the exciting threshold of an artistic life. And he is right.

It is hard to know how close he was to his family at this point. He refers to them occasionally. In October 1901 he hoped his father would come to Birmingham for his 20th birthday, but both he and his father were ill and the visit was cancelled. Happily, his mother sent him one of her "inimitable sponge cakes". Some years later he wrote of going home for Christmas, and later still he also mentioned that he had been home for three weeks.

Unfortunately Max was not good at including dates in his journal so the order in which he did things is often unclear or a matter for guesswork.

In his diary he occasionally included little observations apropos of something he noticed. Sometimes these are funny, sometimes thought-provoking like this one:

*"Quite a number of people have thought that the dead have an influence over the living. How is it that no one has ever said that we have influence over the dead? I see just as much reason in one as in the other."*

Activities included ice skating, walking, making Christmas cards, playing the violin (and sometimes the zither), ping-pong and a popular game called *Up Jenkins*. He hated the latter with a vengeance and seethed with anger when he could not avoid having to play it at some social get-together. He noted his opinion of the game in his diary: *"It is astonishing what a little it takes to make some people yell with laughter. Could hardly get out of the house."*

It was probably much more amusing to spend time with, amongst others, William Bidlake, an architect who lectured at the School of Art, and who was ambidextrous and could draw with both hands simultaneously.

What Max wanted to do – and did – was to attend many talks, recitals, concerts and performances. But we do not know what he made of being one of many students, and it seems likely that he preferred his own company or that of a few close friends. Throughout his life friends – and, obviously, Constance, whom this narrative is now nearing – were clearly highly important to him, and in Birmingham at least, there seemed to be an overlap between fellow students and his lecturers such as Arthur Gaskin and Henry Payne. From time to time he mentions women, such as *"Miss Lewis: she is a divine creature"*. But who was Miss Lewis? One day she came to tea in the studio, and things were "alright" but "the cream was a bit sour". However, he had started on a portrait and on that very day he made a start on her hair and sleeve.

*13*

# David's Mother Plans to Return to Scotland

*Mount Boppy, Canbelego*
*Summer 1912*

After William's death Annie tried to pick up her life in Canbelego. But she could not. Her sole reason for being in Australia had been William, and now he was gone. She found herself thinking more and more about her parents and her home in Scotland. She had lived in Greenock her entire life until she married. So what was she doing in Canbelego? Surely it was time to return to Greenock? While a few of the women advised her to stay and make a life for herself there in Australia, most recommended her to go home to her parents. Annie agreed that the latter was the better option.

But she was full of anxiety about travelling to the other side of the world with two young boys and no one to help her. James was now thirteen and David was eight. The next available ship was not sailing for several weeks, but she booked tickets to a port in England she had never been to and had hardly heard of: Tilbury.

Their journey to Greenock would involve carriages, trains and a ship. The very thought of it exhausted her and as the departure day approached she found herself ill with fear. What if one of the boys fell overboard? Or what if she was seasick? When she had been sick before she had wanted to die, but William had looked after her. And she was anxious too about how, once she had sailed across most of the world, she would find her way from Tilbury to Greenock. William had always taken care of all arrangements when they travelled.

And what should she take with her? Should she take furniture? Or clothes? She and William had married in New South Wales with only a few guests. They had not expected the sort of presents they might have had if they had married in Scotland, and they had not received any. So she packed up two cases, making sure she did not forget her precious painting book with the watercolours she had enjoyed painting. At least this would help her parents to get an idea of Canbelego.

And would she herself then forget Canbelego? And did that matter? And might she even forget William? She was certainly not forgetting him yet, for when the boys were asleep she could still hear him singing the *Skye Boat Song* to her. It made her cry every time she thought about it:

*Skye Boat Song*

*"Speed bonnie boat like a bird on the wing*
*Onward the sailors cry.*

*Carry the lad that's born to be king*
*Over the sea to Skye*

*Loud the wind howls, Loud the waves roar*
*Thunderclaps rend the air*

*Baffled our foes stand by the shore*
*Follow they will not dare*

*Speed bonnie boat like a bird on the wing*
*Onward the sailors cry.*

*Carry the lad that's born to be king*
*Over the sea to Skye."*

There was often an uncertain delay between posting a letter in Canbelego and its arrival in Greenock. Annie could never be sure when – or if – her letters reached her parents or if theirs reached her. But at last she received a brief note from her mother which confirmed that she was expecting Annie and the boys before the end of the month. Annie wept with relief. As each day passed she became more sure that she would not remain in or return to Canbelego.

# Connie Embarks on Writing

Around the early 1890s Connie was ill for a couple of years and must have missed some schooling, but in 1894 she gained a place at the Birmingham School of Art in Margaret Street. This was the art school that Max would enrol in several years later. Unlike him Connie would be living at home, so have all her domestic needs provided for. She must have loved telling her family about the college, the classes, the staff, and the students. And the work too, of course. The courses taught at the college were just the sort of thing that would excite her: repoussage, metalwork, stained glass, painting, illustration and perhaps wood carving, and more.

As Connie became an adult she found and explored her own world of experiences, some of which differed from those of her family. She was not interested in Di's science, nor in her father's opinions about Shakespeare and Bacon. Maybe she enjoyed his roses. She states in *Crusaders, "My primal desire was for adventure and experience, the more reckless the better."* (Note: at this point women's issues seem to have been quite a way down her list of priorities).

It is not easy to see where Connie's desire for actual recklessness came from, but one can imagine her hurrying along pavements on her crutches, enlisting others to help with bags or steps when she could not manage on her own, greeting almost everyone she met, whether she knew them or not, and occasionally (but not often) causing her mother anxiety. It was as if she wanted to make sure that she did not miss anything and, equally important – that no-one missed her. She was certainly determined that her disability would not prevent her from doing what she wanted to do.

But was she actually reckless? There is nothing obvious about her life that deserves such a word, and the term may be one of the many examples of how, looking back at her young life, she chose to broadcast and exaggerate her own dynamic opinion of herself. In short, it feels more a question of "she who wants to be reckless announces to the world that she is, whether she is or not."

Another small episode which illustrates Connie's verve was at the School of Art when Connie suggested to E. R. Taylor, the well-respected principal of the school (known as "The Headmaster"), that the students should put on a

Christmas entertainment. She said that she would write *"The Lay Figure"*, a play set in an art school. She gained permission to do so, and, true to her word, she wrote it. Though this was not a particularly significant event it was another feather in Connie's cap, and added to her tally of those occasions when she succeeded in getting people in authority to do what she wanted. It does not seem that she manipulated people against their will, though at times she tried to, rather that her vibrant enthusiasm made people want to join in with her plans. She was clearly naturally cheerful and animated. Even as a student she managed to access – and soon became used to accessing – funding, influence, opportunity, friends in high places and advantage in general. In short, she was a powerful young woman, and she became more audacious as she grew into adulthood.

Life at the Birmingham Art School would have been stimulating for her, even though moving around between the rooms, exhibition halls and studios of the iconic Ruskinian Venetian Gothic building built in 1885 would have been difficult. The four floors are linked by narrow corridors, iron landings, steps, railings and even gates. These make progress slow for anyone, let alone someone with a stick who is trying to proceed while clutching a folder full of artwork.

The book-like programme for the School of Art was a detailed publication containing lists of numerous courses, fees and prizes. Today many of those attending art schools hope that they will further their skill and knowledge and become popular creative artists. But art schools at the end of the 1800s had other aims, especially if situated in the heart of a conurbation focused on manufacturing. We do not know whether she went to various different branch schools, or only to the Margaret Street building.

This is the introduction to the Birmingham School of Art programme:

*"It will be seen from this programme that morning, afternoon and evening classes are held at the Central School in 5 days a week, from Sept to June and at 14 of the Branch Schools in 5 evenings a week from Sept to May. The hours of the meeting and the fees are so arranged as to be suited to all classes of the community – craftsmen, designers, manufacturers, purchasers, teachers. The main object of the school is to make workmen better workmen. The subjects of instruction are grouped with this view. They bear directly on the local trades."*

It must have been exciting for Connie to choose her courses, most of which were open to women as well as to men. Not aiming to be a workman, she is likely to have decided on the subjects she liked most, such as embroidery and drawing for book illustration. In terms of fellow students, there would have been a real mix including men and women as well as boys and girls. Many youngsters were apprentices sent by their masters to learn a particular craft.

It may have been at the art school that Connie first appreciated the social advantages that she was fortunate enough to enjoy. While many of her fellow King Edward students had had the same level of education and opportunity as she had, there were probably not many who went on to the School of Art.

# 15

# Women's Movement

There is little mention of Connie in connection with the women's movement, although it was the case that at that time the most significant organisations in respect of women's suffrage were in their early stages and had come to general notice. Mrs Pankhurst founded the Women's Social and Political Union (WSPU) in 1903, but there was no evidence yet of Di or Connie joining either that or the National Union of Women's Suffrage Societies (NUWSS).

However, there was significant civil disorder going on under the heading of the rubric *Deeds Not Words*. Post boxes were set on fire, windows smashed, paintings in galleries slashed. Today it is difficult to imagine the strange combination of despair and hope which led people like the two Smedley sisters to support such conduct and damage, even if they did not actually do it themselves.

Mrs Smedley had brought her girls up to be thoughtful of others, to be constructive, to make the most of their lives. How could they abandon such tenets and behave – according to some – so anti-socially and even *rashly*? It is true that other women like themselves did so (eg Sophia Duleep Singh, Constance Lytton and Millicent Fawcett), for a bourgeois upbringing certainly did not – and does not – guarantee a lifetime of socially acceptable behaviour.

At the heart of feminism was the other important issue that affected women in particular: social class and its impact. Obviously those coming into the world are advantaged or disadvantaged by their social position before they take their first breath. Working class girls and women in the early 1900s had many onerous disadvantages. They, like their successors, had to live their lives accepting – outwardly at least – that they were considered of less worth than men, or at least behaving as if they believed that. To be born female and poor was indeed a disaster: an everyday disaster that many managed or were able to survive but more did not or could not. Connie's contemporaries are likely to have grouped themselves, or been grouped, into traditional class divisions as well as into subject divisions.

Mrs Pankhurst always acknowledged that it was her contact with degraded and despised workhouse girls that was the essence of her militancy. She was adamant that women – *all* women – must have the vote if they were to counteract poverty.

In *Crusaders* (Connie's memoirs published in 1929) there is a description of Connie taking a ride in a carriage to the Albert Hall through aggressive crowds who were participating in one of the Women's Movement demonstrations. At that time she claimed she had respect for the motive of the suffragettes' action and that she wrote daily to the press about these events. But when her carriage, whose occupants included a child, was surrounded by angry men, the child cheerfully said that she felt like a revolutionary going to the guillotine. Rather oddly, this opinion made Connie say she felt proud. Surely she knew that it was the aristocrats, not the revolutionaries, who went to the guillotine? Perhaps this incident was an example of Connie's recklessness, although on that occasion things ended happily when anger subsided and, in silence, she and her companions were offered some violets by one of the angry men, which they accepted gracefully.

A point of further interest in respect of poverty, women and Connie, was that Connie, finding herself and others in danger, appeared to be more affected by the defenceless plight of women "of refined birth and upbringing" than by that of poor, ignorant working class women.

# 16

# Politics

As noted previously, Connie was not closely connected to the women's movement. Unlike Di, despite being in London for most of the time when women were demonstrating and promoting solidarity through the distribution of leaflets and attendance at meetings, Connie does not seem to have taken a particularly active part in the battle for women's emancipation. To be in the midst of that excitement but hardly to engage with it indicates that her life and interests were more personal than political, more private than public. It was really only when she became aware of the impoverished lives of the mill-workers in the Cotswolds that she directed at least some of her energy to improving their lot.

Despite being broadly apolitical, she was asked to speak at an inaugural meeting of the local Liberals. She argued that, unlike other parties (whose manifestos she was not completely familiar with), the Liberals believed in the possibilities of progress. But it seemed as though Connie somehow thought that positive progress would occur all by itself, without people having to do anything about it. Pageants encouraged people to witness how (edited) events followed (other edited) events in neat order, and suggested to audiences that their society was heading towards a better future. Of course, the nature and purpose of pageants required them to end on a hopeful and optimistic note.

One surprising absence in *Crusaders* and other literature and correspondence, is any mention of the American actor and writer Elizabeth Robins who was contemporaneous with Connie. She specialised in playing Ibsen's roles, and her play *Votes for Women* was a big success. It was performed at the Royal Court in April 1907 and it firmly established her feminist credentials. Most of Act 2 of the play portrays a public demonstration, from which these few lines are taken from a speech given by *A Working Woman*:

*"W'y does any woman tyke less wyges than a man for the same work? Only because we can't get anything better. That's part the reason w'y we're yere to-d'y. Do you reely think we tyke them there low wyges because we got a lykin' for low wyges? No. We're just like you. We want as much as ever we can get. ("'Ear! 'Ear!" and laughter.) We got a gryte deal to do with our wyges, we women has. We got the children to think about."*

Though she was American Elizabeth Robins was much more involved with the feminist organisations in the capital than was Connie, being a member of the NUWSS and the WSPU, and giving talks for them. She also gave talks about the theatre. For example, in the centenary year of Ibsen's death she gave a lecture on *"Ibsen and the Actress"*. Even if she was far more worldly than the rather younger Connie one can imagine the pair greatly enjoying each other's company. They would have talked books and writing, and would have found plenty to laugh about. It was a pity if it was the case that they did not meet.

# 17

# Connie Spreads Her Wings

Beginning early in the twentieth century, Connie published forty books, about twenty of them novels and the rest plays, children's books, and non-fiction. She also wrote a polemical feminist manifesto and much later she wrote *Crusaders*, her book of memoirs. Writing was only one aspect of her career. In addition, her theories about the theatre, teaching, and practice (writing and directing plays and pageants, not all of them published or produced), were sometimes connected with her work in the visual arts such as embroidery, illustration, even dance.

By the time she left the Birmingham School of Art in around 1902 she was already thinking about writing novels. Many first novels never reach the light of day, but this was not the case for Connie, for she was fortunate enough to receive interest, publication and, one assumes, payment within a very short time.

The chief theme of *The April Princess,* Connie's first real success, is a princess's attempts at exposing the folly of her conventional aunt's point-of-view. In both style and content Connie was trying to throw convention away and open readers up to her novel depiction of wit, self-confidence and character. In much of her work she likes to imagine herself as a storybook princess.

Here is a scene-setting quote:

*"The sun beat down on the Princess's head and the Princess looked up and laughed. Its light was so fierce and strong that the Princess soon closed her eyes again, but she laughed still. Today was the Princess's birthday and the Princess's aunt with whom she lived, had seen fit to deliver a few remarks to her niece upon the subject of discretion, in which she considered the Princess was lacking.*

*'I have been hoping to see your flippancy become chastened as your years advance but instead of improving you seem to become more frivolously irresponsible each year,' said the aunt. 'When you were sixteen you gave promise of a serious and intellectual bent of mind'."*

In the opening paragraph of this very short example, it seems odd that Connie uses the word "princess" six times. Writing like that, of course, cements the presence and character of the Princess, which is presumably what she wants to happen. Or were her books not edited?

In short, her work earned good reviews despite the fact that some of them consisted mostly of rather repetitive dialogue, annoying characters and had little in the line of plot. Some were written in what – to some readers – could be described as tiresome and artificial voices. Despite this, her work was clearly enjoyed by many and the fact that a New York publisher decided to publish one must have thrilled Connie. To get one's first novel published in the USA: some trophy!

*18*

# Connie Continues Writing

*The April Princess* was the first book in which Connie mentioned her "Kingdom". This was the name of a suspension-of-disbelief feature, straight out of a folk tale. The Kingdom appeared often, and provided the scenes for her narratives. It was territory where reality and imagination crossed over, and where actual people in her life were given names and roles. It is difficult, today, to understand how Connie's friends and family agreed to be part of her phantom world. She was called by the name Princess at art school, but was that because she was just a popular girl whose friends did what she wanted to humour her? She openly advertised the fact that she wished she could translate her imaginary life and its fictional characters into reality. Surely some people – including her family – must have thought this very bizarre, not to say juvenile? And surely she wanted her body to be made whole?

However, the book was very popular and its success was perhaps mostly due to the fact that it seemed to create some sort of cult. Some of the factors criticised previously were the very ones which many readers enjoyed most. Connie's inclusion of unusual words such as "absquatulated" must have amused people, and it is not difficult to imagine her friends (probably mostly female ones) talking to each other about this one-off wacky and, at times, other-worldly writer.

Another trademark feature of Connie's writing at this times was her sharp feminist awareness which occasionally cut into her texts.

This example is from *Crusaders*:

*"We cheerfully admit that we are just as human as men and are universally deciding to come down to the level of his comrades and his equals."*

And this is from *The April Princess*:

*"'I wish you would understand that love is of no more importance to me than it is to a man, and I hope I will be in love just as many times and in as many different ways,' she added with a side glance to see the effect of this bold and startling statement on the Quiet Man."*

*51*

One of the early books had the dynamic title: *Woman – a Few Shrieks*. Using an epistolary style, addressed to certain imagined characters, Connie promoted feminism in an amusing and provocative way.

In 1907, Olive Schreiner, a South African who was very strongly committed to feminism, included these words in one of the nearly five thousand letters she wrote:

*"Have you read a most splendid thing called 'Woman – a few Shrieks', by a Miss Smedley? The humour is grand."*

And Connie had some words of wisdom, too:

*"After all it's so stupid to hate oneself! You've got to live with yourself when all's said and done."*

By contrast, it was around this time (1907) when Connie became involved in discussions about Kenneth Grahame's *Wind in the Willows*. Somehow her influence enabled Grahame to get a publisher. Many had turned it down, but Theodore Roosevelt's approval secured its future.

Connie's parents must have enjoyed her excitement and literary success, though one cannot help wondering what they – and William, in particular – thought of her work. His book *The Mystery of Bacon* was well-written, indeed scholarly, while his daughter's books were (at least at this early period of her development) quirky and written in the simple and repetitive way described above. Of course William's book about Bacon cannot be compared, for example, with Connie's one entitled *Beau and Belle*, for they were attempting to do completely different jobs. We should probably conclude that William was an indulgent father, rightly pleased that his daughter, about whose life he and his wife had such concern, was getting on with and enjoying something worthwhile, and already being recognised for it.

It is quite probable that neither Connie, nor Di nor Billie read more than a few pages of the book that had cost their father so much time, energy and commitment.

Connie's early books, such as *The April Princess, The Boudoir Critic, For Heart o'Gold* and *Conflict* feel very autobiographical, for the main character in many of them is a young woman who seems to closely resemble Connie herself. Was it that connection which readers liked? If not, what was it, exactly, that brought her so much praise?

(At the back of this book there is a list of many of Connie's books.)

Duckworth was the publisher for a good number of them – notably *Crusaders* – and the reason for that was, at least in part, because not only did the company know her, but that its relationship with her was strong and active. Indeed, Connie's mother was born a Duckworth, and Connie was the godmother of a Duckworth baby in New Zealand.

Many of her other books were published by Chatto and Windus, thanks to the strong friendship that existed between her and the influential Geoffrey Whitworth. He was a lecturer and author, editor of the Christian Science Monitor and future founder of the British Drama League.

Today, with important exceptions, it is unusual for a novelist to employ a great deal of dialogue, but it was clearly Connie's delight in dialogue which pushed her towards playwriting. Her novels could almost be considered to be plays, but few would describe them or her actual plays as dramatic in the sense of 'full of drama' or, at least, what counts for drama today. And despite the fact that *The April Princess*, a novel in prose, attracted so much attention and praise, Connie's attention soon turned even more to drama. Once interested in a new type of activity, she wasted no time in exploring it. Not only did she write plays for the stage, but she became interested in acting techniques and movement and all that goes with production and performance: music, costume, speech and more. She would build on these experiences later on.

Simultaneously she began to made contact with actors such as Charles Wyndham, a very popular player who performed in melodrama and comedy. But how did she do this without, seemingly, any contacts? It appears as if some introductions came through the social events Connie's family provided or attended, and others through approaching people she wanted to talk to, as bold as brass. It is not hard to imagine her capitalising on chance encounters or looking up from her crutches at a stage door, boldly and baldly announcing that, say, Mrs Pat (aka Mrs Patrick Campbell) was expecting her, and the doorman rather nervously allowing Connie in, believing that deference was his best course of action.

Connie was a natural networker. Inspired by whatever project was in hand, she rarely agreed to settle for a negative response from whoever she was trying to get something from. She was prepared to challenge to achieve her purpose, as well as to work hard. At times she might well have been so enthusiastic or indignant or earnest about whatever her current concerns were that conversation with her would be rather both tiring and annoying. Nevertheless, *Crusaders* names a number of influential people she found a way of meeting. Some are actors or artists or writers, such as Alice Meynell, or Gertrude Hudson. Others are members of the aristocracy. A good number are not English. Connie, it seems, set out to impress people with titles and important positions. And why not? Why should she not seek help – financial or otherwise? It seems that she did not do this because she wanted to improve her social status (a charge which she could be accused of) but in order to achieve her real aim: getting another project on the road. Another explanation for her ability to engage the support of others might be the (unmentioned) fact that people felt sorry for her disability. In short, they wanted to help, either because they pitied her, or because doing so made them feel good, or a mixture of both of these, and, obviously, they themselves gained satisfaction from completing something well.

Edward McKnight Kauffer, an American, was the sort of art-connected person Connie liked to be friends with. In the early 1900s he specialised in creating posters to advertise London Underground at a time when travelling by steam-driven tube trains was becoming very popular. McKnight Kauffer was interested in other art forms too, and Max painted and sketched his portrait in 1915.

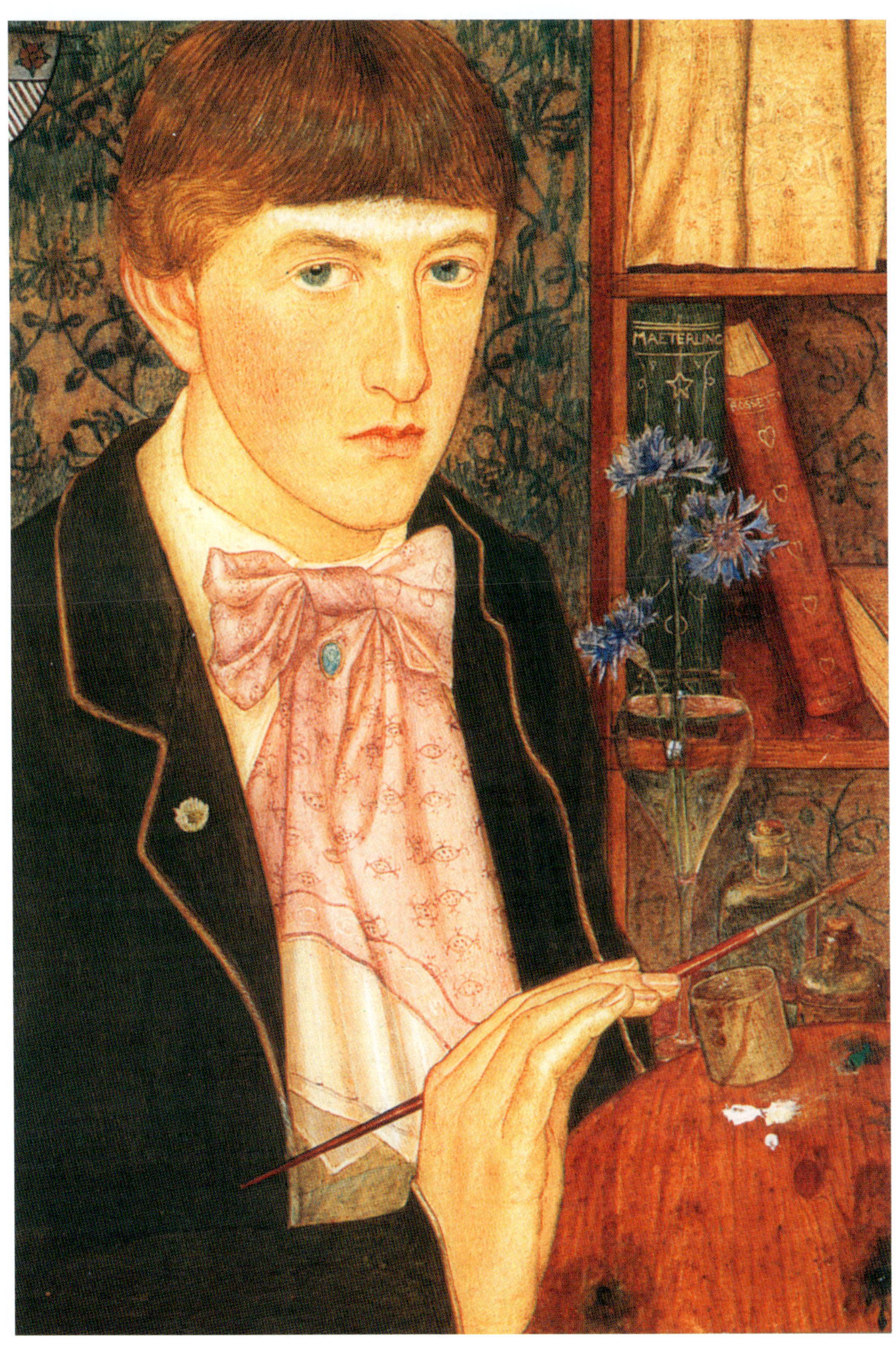

*Max's 'Self Portrait'.*

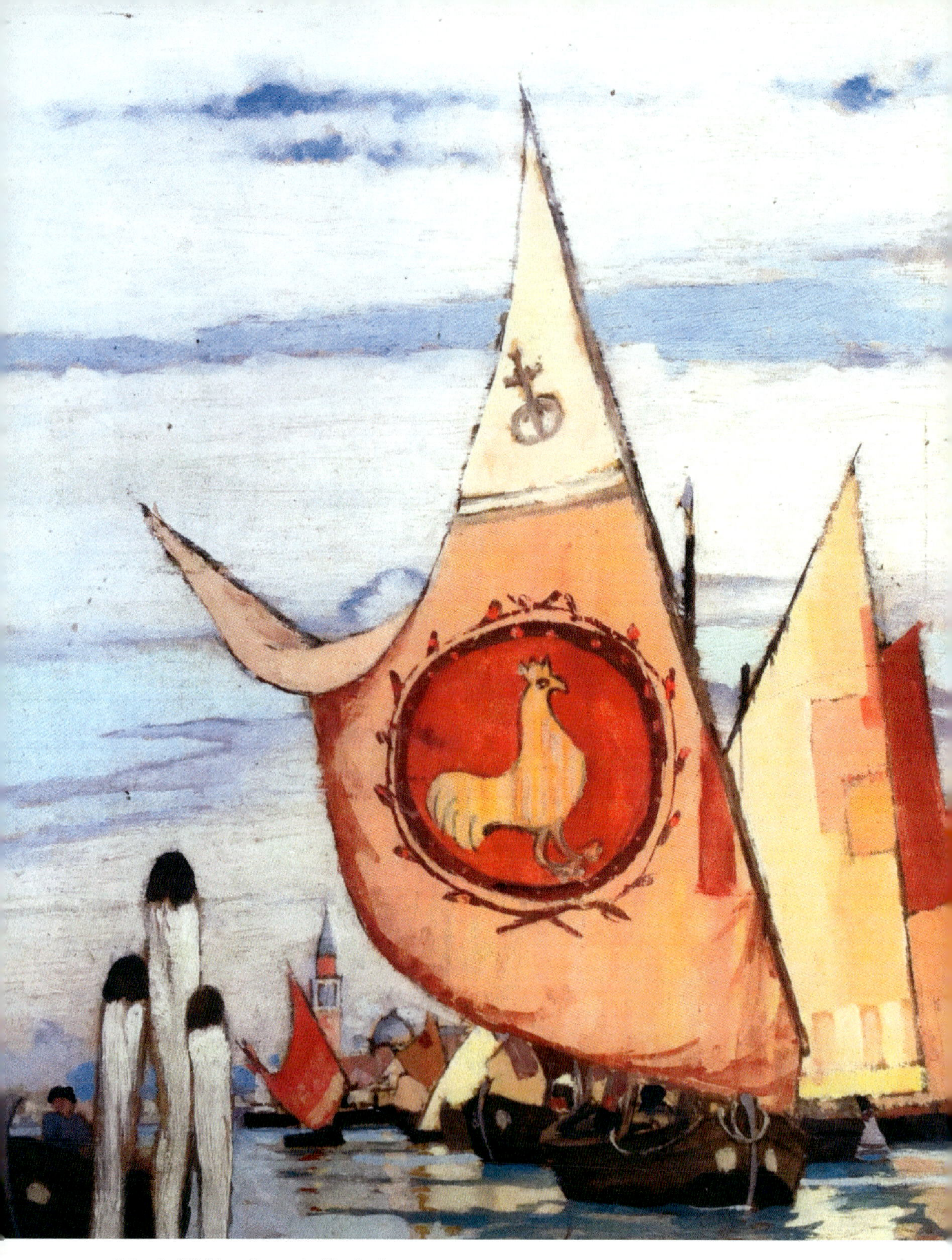

*Max's 'Fishing Boats in Venice'.*

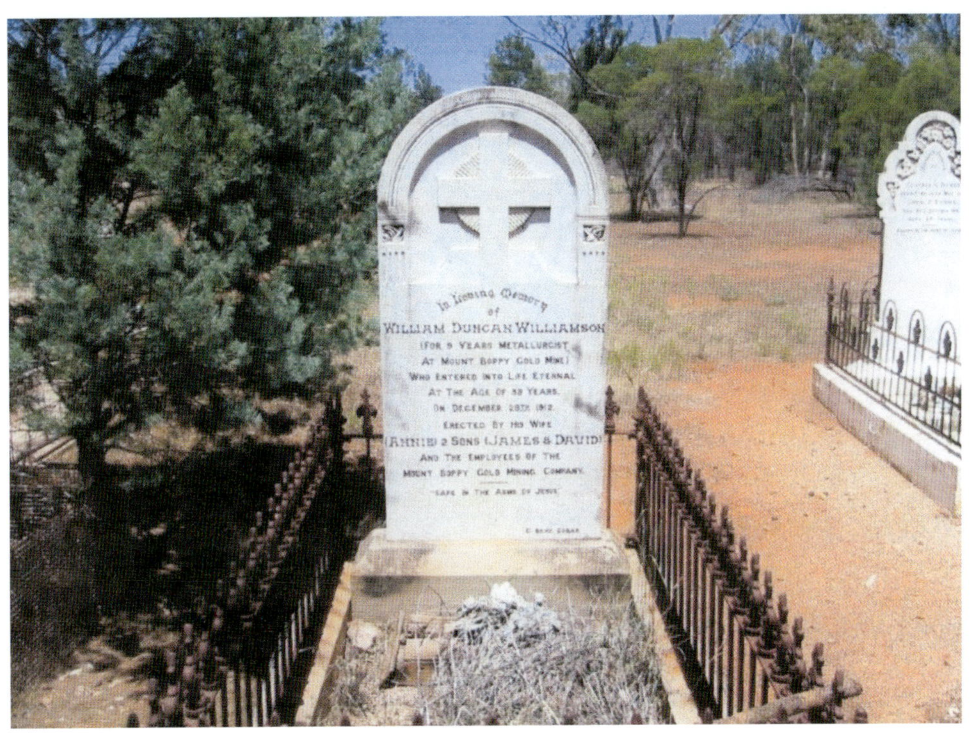

*William Williamson's grave near Mount Boppy, Canbelego.*

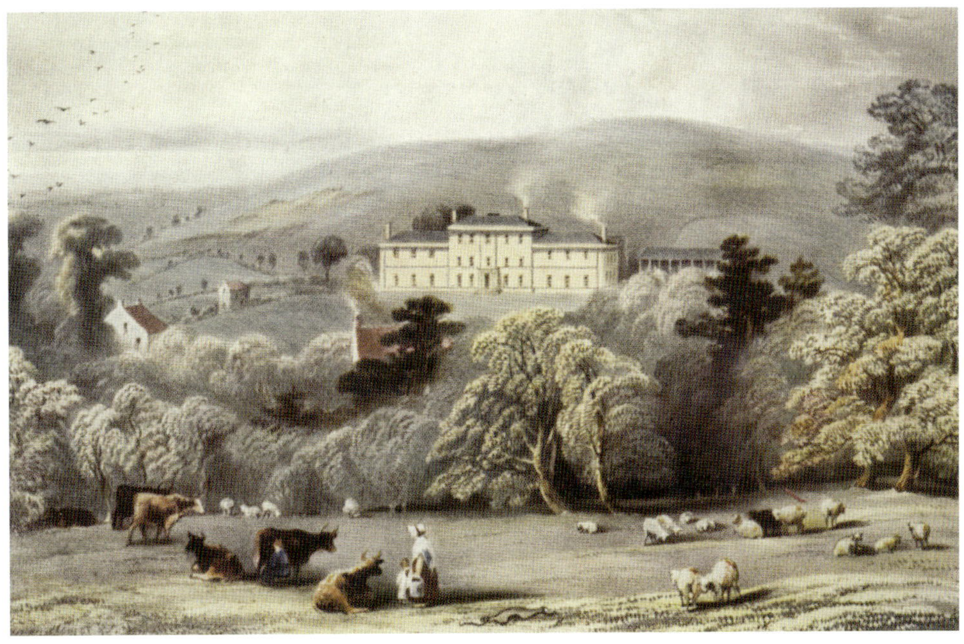

*Sidcot School, 1838 by William Arnee Frank.*

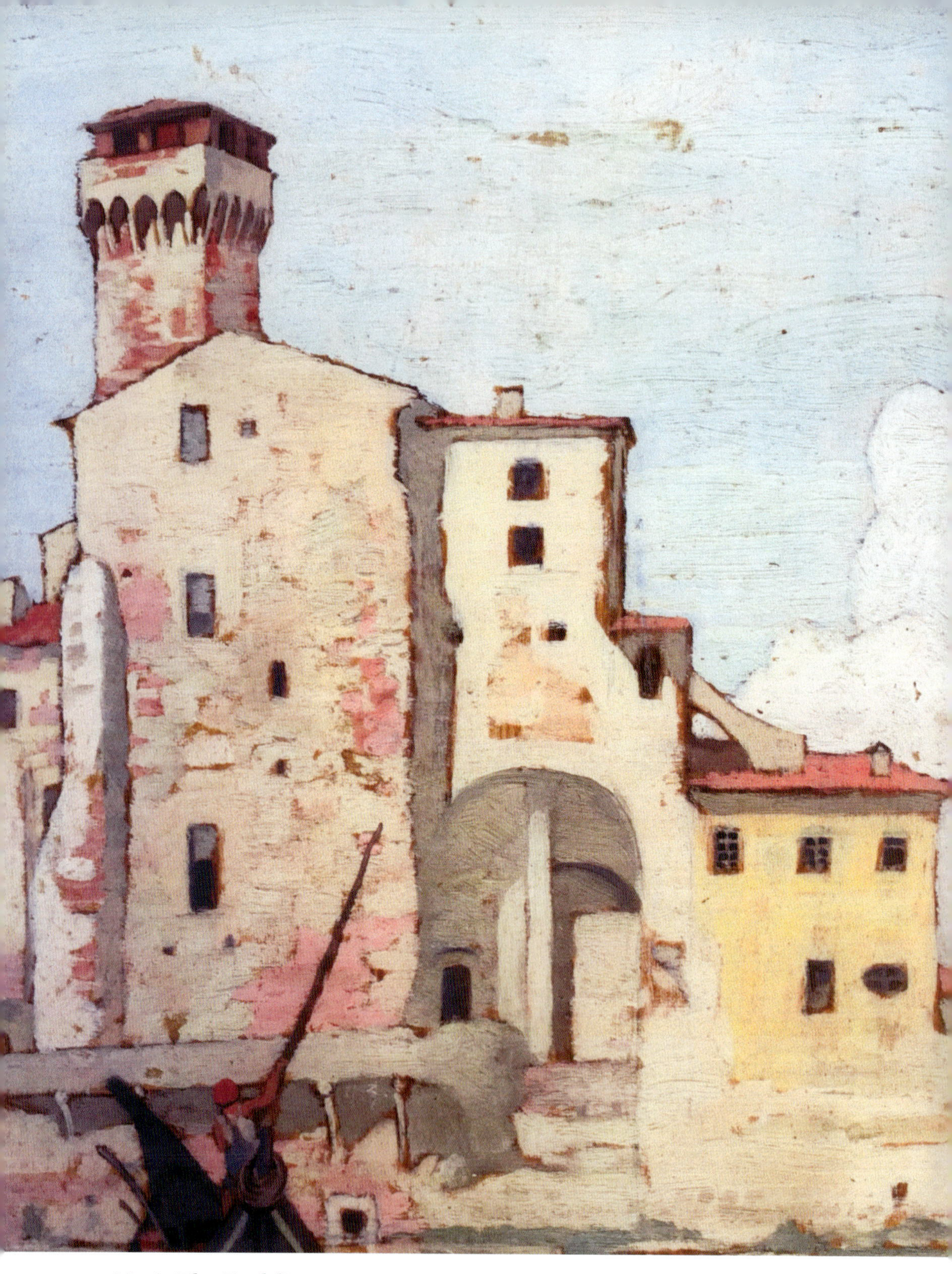

*Max's 'The Citadel'.*

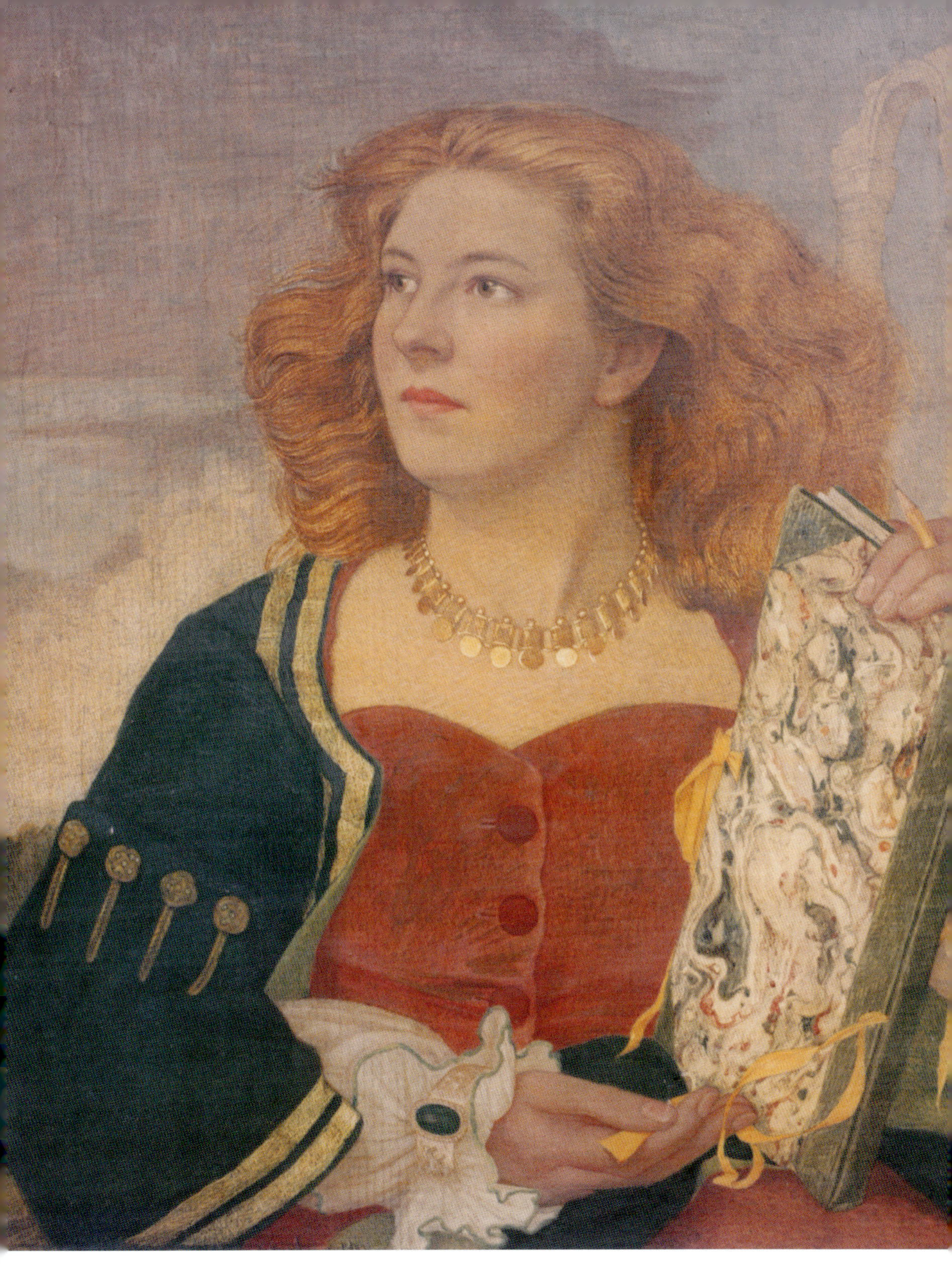

*Max's 'Portrait of Diana Armfield'.*

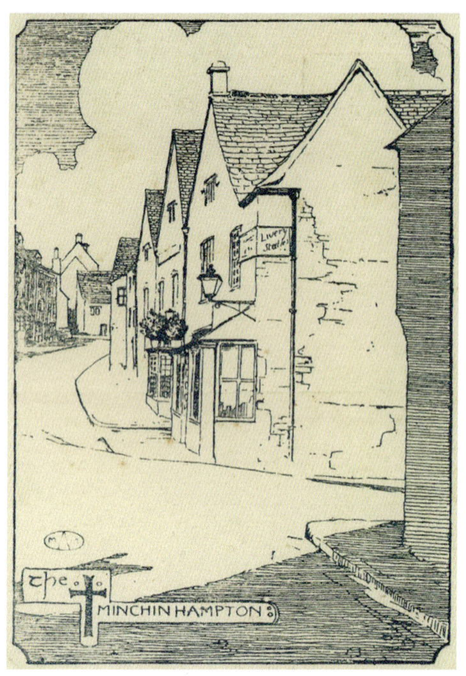

*Cotswolds scene by Max.*

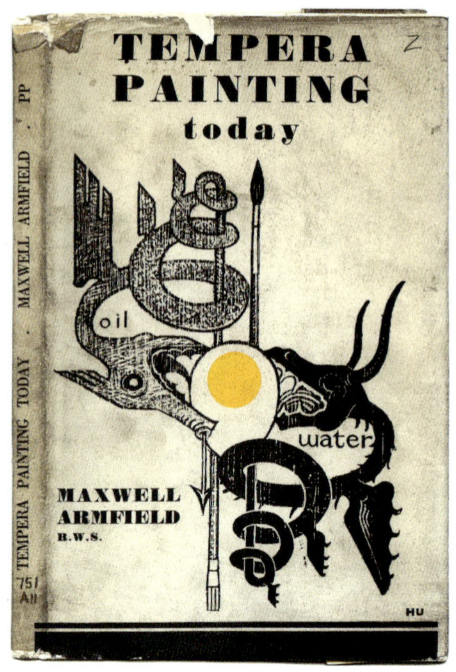


*Max's cover of 'Tempera Painting Today'.*

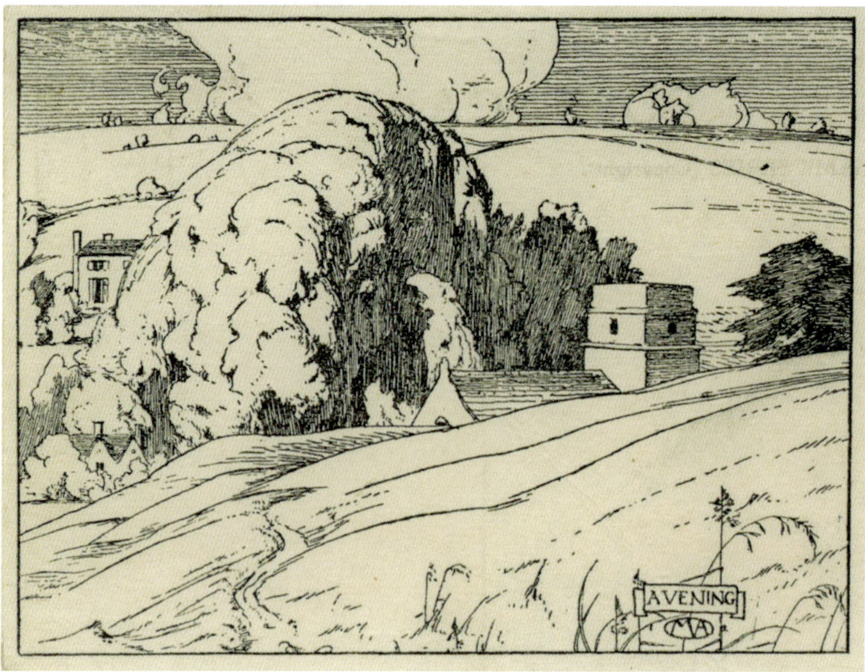


*Cotswolds scene by Max.*

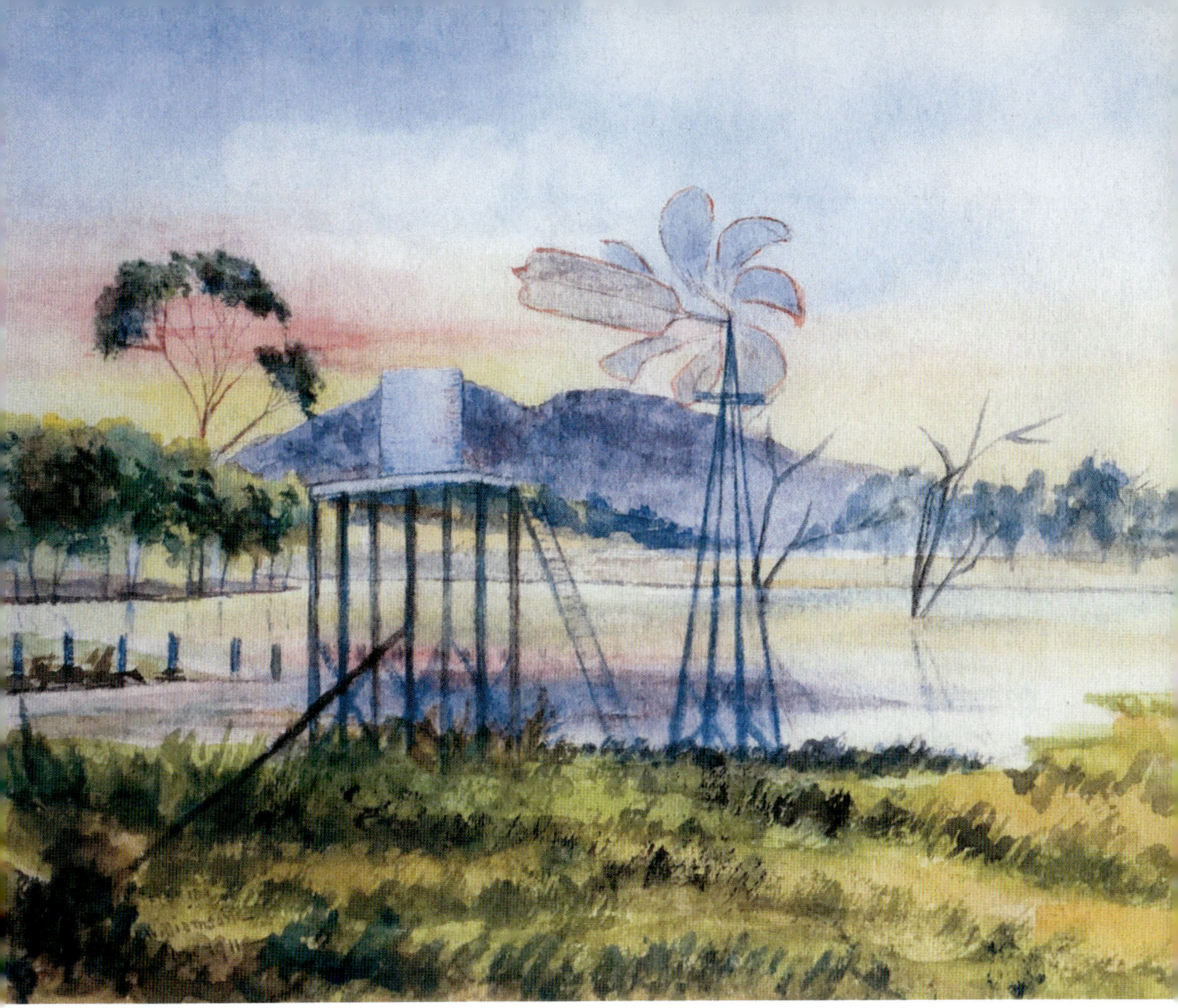

Annie's watercolour of sheep station, Canbelego.

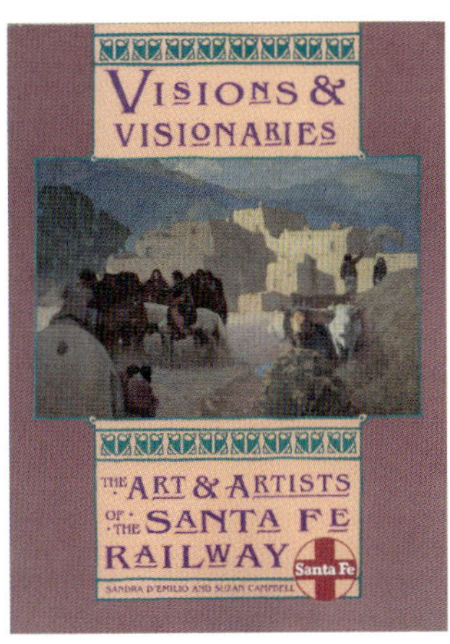

Cover from 'Visions &
Visionaries'.

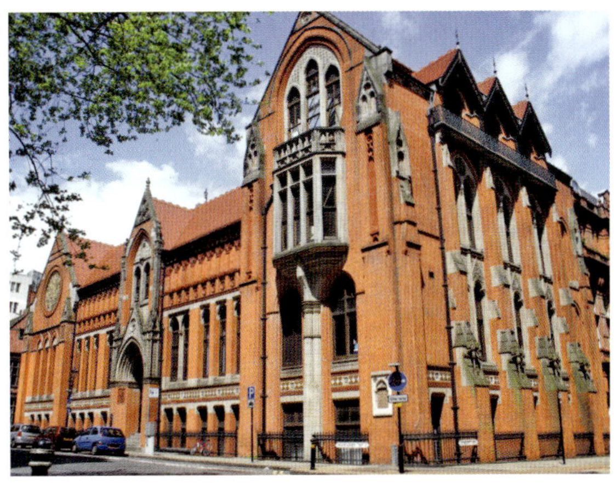

Birmingham Art School.

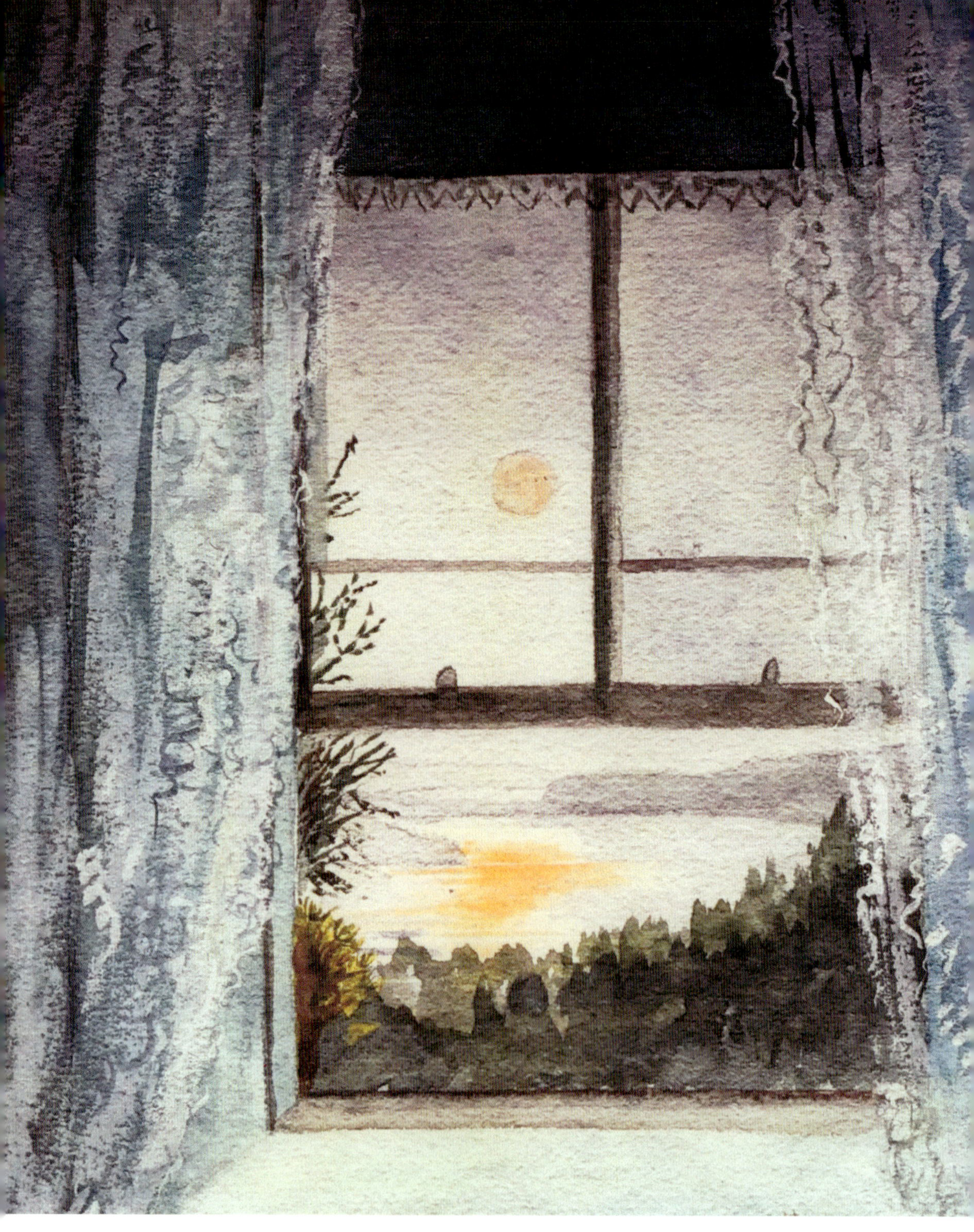

*Annie's watercolour in Scotland.*

VIII

# 19

# The Armfields

When it was time to leave school, Max had to make a decision about his future. Despite his clear interest in art, there was definitely a suggestion or even assumption that he might follow his father into engineering and business. But he had absolutely no wish to do so at all. Some twenty years later, in 1943, he painted a picture of the head of a man against an industrial background. Entitled *This England, Portrait of an Owner*, this portrait was certainly not a portrait of the paternal and gentle Joseph Armfield, but many viewers identify its tension, sharpness, and lack of empathy with hard-headed business: the very opposite of what mattered to Max.

Max's father had a finely balanced, if over-busy life, rather as William Smedley did. As well as being efficient, supportive and creative in his workplace and home he had various other important responsibilities and interests: he was a Justice of the Peace for Hampshire, and he served on the Ringwood Rural District Council and the Board of Guardians. He was the Chairman of the Council of School Governors and of the New Forest Liberal Association, and the founder of the local branch of the League of Nations Union. All of these interests would have enabled him to take a wide and generous view of the opportunities that were open to Max in respect of earning a living, contributing to the public good and fulfilling his own potential.

> TO
>
> JOSEPH AND MARGARET ARMFIELD
>
> WHO EARLY TAUGHT ME
> THE USE OF TOOLS AND
> THE LOVE OF BEAUTY
> WHICH ARE THE FIRST
> NECESSITIES OF THE
> CRAFTSMAN

*Dedication in Rhythmic Shape.*

Joseph Armfield also found time to take photos, and paint. Diana Armfield told me that each year, as the summer ended, Joseph's whole family made plans as to what they were going to do when winter approached and life became more interior. Many of these plans were to paint and sketch, and every individual joined in. Max wrote that no-one could have had more encouragement from their family. When younger he must have enjoyed the small sketches that Joseph often drew for him on his letters.

The following, written by Diana Armfield, indicates that as well as going to his home at Heron Court in Ringwood, he liked to visit some of his other relations at Oaktree House:

*"Maxwell, who, as a young man, had emancipated himself from Heron Court, visited Oaktree at fairly regular intervals. His visits were looked forward to, my mother having not only a real affection for him but she also possessed a romantic admiration for artists, hence her easily won pleasure at my marrying one!"*

Diana not only became an artist herself, but she married Bernard Dunstan, who was also an artist. She is perhaps best known for her paintings of flowers and landscapes, but she also paints portraits, literary subjects and still lifes.

*20*

# David Moves to Scotland

Annie arrived in Greenock to find her parents looking older. They were astonished by their grandsons who filled the house, were always hungry and who spoke in an unfamiliar accent. The boys got on fine at school but at the end of 1917 James began to have periods of pain and sickness. He became ill and the various medicines he took did not improve things.

Within a month he was dead. He was buried on January 6th 1919.

(There are also others in the family who believe that James was buried in Japan. If that was the case, he could have died when on board with his mother and David, and buried when – or if – their ship had sailed to Scotland via Japan.)

Annie, surely deeply damaged by her misfortunes, painted more scenes. She went to Whiting Bay in Arran, and Tarbet, and Gareloch and more. Sometimes she opened her book at the beginning and looked through the paintings she had done of Canbelego, but sometimes she shut her eyes. She could not bear the fact that William, with whom she had so often walked around those lakes and past those trees was missing. She tried to imagine him in the scenes she had painted. Standing by the lake, perhaps, or leaning against a post. She recalled vividly that soon after she and William had moved to Canbelego she had become pregnant, and they used to like strolling together slowly. And now James and David existed, but her dearest, dearest William did not.

But Annie found that painting helped, and she soon filled all the remaining pages of her book. A sea scene she was particularly pleased with carried a title on the back: *View looking east from drawing room window, 54 Union Street, Greenock.* She liked the way how, in one of them, the lighthouse, though small, was right in the centre.

She still heard William singing *My love is like a red, red rose:*

*A Red, Red Rose*

*O my Luve is like a red, red rose*
   *That's newly sprung in June;*
*O my Luve is like the melody*
   *That's sweetly played in tune.*

*So fair art thou, my bonnie lass,*
   *So deep in luve am I;*
*And I will luve thee still, my dear,*
   *Till a' the seas gang dry.*

*Till a' the seas gang dry, my dear,*
   *And the rocks melt wi' the sun;*
*I will love thee still, my dear,*
   *While the sands o' life shall run.*

After leaving school David attended the University of Glasgow where he studied electrical engineering. He was selected as an apprentice at Metropolitan Vickers where his keenness, intelligence and industry were noted. He completed his training in 1929 and was transferred to the company's engineering staff in Sheffield, and would, later on in 1942, join the staff of the Institution of Electrical Engineers in London.

His mother Annie re-married, but David and his new step-father did not get on well, and his relationship with his family diminished. He had lost his father and his brother, and now felt distant from his mother.

# 21

# Max at Birmingham School of Art

Max, as has been shown, was used to artists and painting. It was no surprise that he turned away from manufacturing and towards the arts. However, he was well aware that his father would have wanted him to take over the family business, and he was reluctant to upset him by declining to do so. He cannot have felt good when he turned down, as apparently he did, his father's alternative suggestion that he should go to Oxford. Happily for Max, Joseph Armfield cared more for his son's wishes than for his own. It was certainly to Max's advantage that his father was interested in much more than his ironworks. At nineteen, Max clearly did not share his father's hopes in respect of a career, but looking ahead at his unfolding life, he must have been boosted by Joseph Armfield's generous confidence in him as an artist. His father, too, would have realised that Max was never going to make a business man.

These things are confirmed by the warm letters from his father, such as this extract, which seems to have been written just days before Max actually left school:

*July 19 1899*

*My dear Maxwell,*

*The time is drawing near now when we hope to see you home and then your school days will I suppose be ended though not the time for learning. That extends through life.*

*I daresay mother had told you that we have written to Birmingham and received a lot of particulars about the Municipal School of Art that I hope may be useful though it will no doubt be difficult to decide exactly what it is best to do for the first term and it maybe that after attending there you may be able to form a better opinion of what branches or courses of study it is best for you. There is a downside to Birmingham as no doubt there is to every place. It is not a nice place to have to live in.*

Did they choose this School because it was not in London, which Max would have had little knowledge of? Or because the Birmingham School of Art had a very good reputation? Either way, Birmingham was an excellent choice. It was one of the leading art schools in the country and one of the first in the UK to be municipally funded, though there had been a government-funded school in the city since 1843. Purpose-built, it had opened in 1885, and it definitely had prestige. It is recorded in an art school magazine, *The Art Student*, that Edward Burne-Jones gave tutorials to some of the more advanced students at the School in 1885, and speakers at the annual prize-giving included William Morris.

Its reputation was – and still is – closely connected to that particular individual artist: William Morris. Born in 1834 he became a designer and craftsman in numerous specialisms: ceramics, embroidery, typography, illuminated manuscripts and more. He was largely self-taught, and was fortunate enough to inherit a substantial fortune which enabled him to make art, to travel and to write without the need to earn money. He was also a poet, and a socialist who worked for associations such as the Social Democratic Foundation. In his last years, he founded the legendary Kelmscott Press where he produced over fifty beautiful books before he died in 1896.

Morris threw himself into life with generosity and energy, and his long friendship with the artist and designer Edward Burne-Jones cemented his passion for art and learning and, extremely importantly, his political interests. He was a key figure in the Arts and Crafts Movement and its focus on decoration, but it was Morris's impressive skills, optimistic attitude and his hopes and fears for society that enabled him to do so much so well for so long.

Max and his family might perhaps not have known much about him before making the decision to enrol at the School of Art, but it turned out to be an extremely good step forward.

So, it can be assumed that, in 1899 or 1900, at eighteen years of age, Max went off to Birmingham with Joseph and Margaret's financial support as well as their blessing. Perhaps he also had a few letters of introduction. Though money hardly gets a mention in the diaries it was the case that his parents gave him an adequate and regular amount until well into his adult life. However, there were many times when he made urgent requests for more, both from his father and (later on) from Harold, his younger brother who eventually took over the family business. At the end of his life he even asked for money – and received it, from his sister-in-law Ida.

But what did this household of young men do about food and laundry? Max and his fellow students went to very inexpensive restaurants, and probably relied on a maid to change the sheets and keep the place clean. We can be almost certain that there were servants in their own homes, so life would have been different for Max and his friends when they had to provide for and look after their own needs. However, Max gained an advantage when, in some new accommodation he won – by the toss of a coin – the reward of accommodation in a room right next door to the studio, meaning that he did not have to live at a distance. Between them, the students were probably perfectly successful in creating a lifestyle that suited their interests, their attendance at college and their budgets.

In imagining his life in Birmingham, one must try to acknowledge how very different things would have been both from Max's family home at Ringwood and from his boarding school. He shared a studio with artists Charles Gere and Henry Payne, both serious students. Three young men and their painting materials must have taken up quite a lot of space. Both Payne and Gere were stained glass designers, while Payne was a water-colourist who also worked on frescoes, and Gere illustrated books and designed embroidery. An important friend and influence was Joseph Southall from whom he learned much.

In *Tempera Painting Today* he writes:

*"I myself use tempera when it seems suitable to convey what is required precisely as I choose to use a gimlet or a bradawl or a brace and bit according to the type of hole I wish to make."*

Charles Dickens in *Pickwick Papers*, described poverty well and some of his characters visited plenty of areas that neither Connie or Max was likely to explore:

*"As they rattled through the narrow thoroughfares leading to the heart of the turmoil, the sights and sounds of earnest occupation struck more forcibly on the senses. The streets were thronged with working people. The hum of labour resounded from every house; lights gleamed from the long casement windows in the attic storeys and the whirl of wheels and the noise of machinery shook the trembling walls. The fires, whose lurid sullen light had been visible for miles, blazed fiercely up in the great works and factories of the town. The din of hammers, the rushing of steam, and the dead heavy clanking of engines, was the harsh music which arose from every quarter." (Charles Dickens, The Posthumous Papers of Mr Pickwick, 1837.)*

These images would be quite familiar to Max, albeit on a far smaller scale. Though Ringwood might have seemed big to a local inhabitant it was the tiniest of workshops when compared with the dragons that breathed fire inside Birmingham.

Another difference Max would have noted would have been that, unlike in Ringwood, the inhabitants of Birmingham came from a wide range of countries, such as China, the West Indies, Asia and Ireland. Later, he would come to use some of what he saw about him in his figures, portraits and in their costumes.

In a booklet entitled *The History of Moseley Hall*, researched and compiled by John Innes, is a journalist's brief account of a popular Birmingham jamboree:

*"… the chief event of the year was the Bicycle Gymkhana which was held annually, usually towards the end of June. The account of the 1901 event, in the Birmingham Pictorial and Dart (a contemporary local paper) is of interest in that it reveals what may seem strange to us today, when so many people of 'ethnic minorities' have been welcomed into our society. Clearly the sight of a dark-skinned person in those days was so unusual as to merit reporting in the press:*

*As I approached the flag-decorated entrance to Moseley Hall, a cyclist with a dark face and a bright red scarlet turban dashed past and joined the well dressed throng at the gate. I thought for a moment that some of the competitors were riding through the streets in costume, but on closer inspection I discovered that he was a genuine Hindu. Subsequently I obtained an introduction and made a sketch which he signed J. M. Cotelingam. The ladies made much of him."*

We have already seen that Connie and Max came from creative, socially aware and philanthropic parents whose endeavours were financially successful and personally fulfilling. Now, quite separately, each of the talented pair was on that exhilarating threshold of the next stage of their life.

Max moved from his studio and found somewhere to live in Edgbaston, one of the most attractive parts of Birmingham. It was the location of the famous cricket ground which had been created in 1882, just one year after he was born. (The Aston Villa football club was founded in 1874, and Birmingham City in 1943), but it is doubtful that Max had any interest in playing or watching sport.) The previous owners of the land in Edgbaston had refused to allow any industry or commerce to take place there, thus rendering it desirable and healthy to live in – if one could afford it, as Max could.

Birmingham was growing fast. There were plenty of opportunities to see plays, circuses and music halls but Max made the most of those which could be called high-brow. Theatrical events could be seen at the Curzon Hall, the Gaiety, the Empire, and there was also the Alexandra Theatre which opened in 1901 as a cinema under the name of the Lyceum – a name which will feature soon as a very different and important part of this story.

Other than working on his art, Max indulged his strong interest in literature, drama and music, for he was really hungry to be a creative artist rather than a spectator or listener. He occasionally created musical compositions "with which I amuse myself at odd moments". He joined an orchestra and kept up his violin playing. He read poetry voraciously. Reading the journal entries, it feels as if he had decided that he would not waste a minute: rather like his father.

Max started to keep a journal in 1901, the beginning of his first year in Birmingham. The early entries reveal that he was already an active artist. He was working on two illustrations: *The Life and Death of Jason* and on *Rugby Footballers.*

Importantly, he completed a self-portrait in 1901. This shows him as a young man determined to present a flattering portrait of himself and to attract attention. In the portrait he has a paint brush in his hand, but he does not really look as if he is ready to paint. He is facing the viewer but not looking at him or her directly. The whole picture feels delicate, and though Max is close to his hardly seen easel (or perhaps it is just a table?), there is little of the traditional artist about him, and the room seen by the viewer is as much like a sitting room as a studio. This impression is partly because of the way he is dressed, for he has chosen his clothes with care. He wears a simple dark jacket trimmed with pale edging, and, dramatically, a contrasting big, pink, soft silk bow at his neck. A cornflower in a vase echoes his bright blue eyes. To make sure that viewers understand who he is and what matters to him, he has made visible the spines of three books by favourite authors: He has chosen Maurice Maeterlinck (poet, dramatist and essayist), Dante Gabriel Rossetti (painter, illustrator, translator and poet) and John Keats, the Romantic poet who died when very young.

While a student (and later) Max paid great attention to his appearance, and it is easy to imagine people admiring him as he walked down a street. Interestingly, he was described by someone who knew him well as "a sparrow", which indicates a slight, neat body. That was indeed the case though one thinks of a sparrow as a fast mover, and speed does not match with what is known of Max's nature. Though quite able to get things done promptly when necessary, his preferred style was thought through, unhurried and controlled. He was certainly not driven by emotion.

When Connie was 24 and Max was 19 their lives were lived almost entirely in Birmingham. Though it is unlikely that they had heard of each other at that point, it is quite possible that their paths may have crossed. Indeed, Connie wrote that they met at the school of art, but this might not have been the case.

Max, in respect of his own paintings, would surely have endorsed Morris's words, "My work is the embodiment of dreams in one form or another".

It is not difficult to imagine Max smiling as he recognised others rather like himself. We cannot know how often he indulged his sartorial fantasies but it seems unlikely that many young men in 1900 – in Birmingham, at least – dressed as he did. Geoffrey Whitworth commented:

*"He is very quiet in manner, but at the same time has much dignity. He dresses in black velvet, with a silken orange-red bow tie which he has stencilled with patterned in gold."*

There was no doubt about it: Maxwell Armfield wanted to turn heads – and must have done so – on the street as well as in private homes. At some stage he rode a motorbike, and made the most of the opportunity to wear leathers, thus promoting an outré portrait of himself. However, because he was rather embarrassed about being seen by some of his relations in his gleaming black leather outfit, his elegant boots and his dark helmet and gloves he sometimes changed into conventional clothes before knocking on the door.

22

# Start of Lyceum

However she managed to get things done, Connie was almost always having ideas and making them successful. A particularly important one took off in 1902, when she was beginning to be interested in and of interest to writers and actors, publishers and editors, artists and musicians. She had become aware that there was no designated place where professional women could meet in civilised comfort in the way that men could in their clubs. By 1902 she must have invited numerous people to her middle-class home for any number of reasons such as reviewing a new publication, discussing a concert, and listening to classical music. Of course there was a strong social element to such gatherings but despite the warm hospitality that Connie and her parents provided, it became increasingly clear that she could not continue to use her family home, or even parts of it, as either an office, or a meeting hall or a cafe, let alone all three. Supportive as they were, the family must have complained at times about the number of comings and goings, and it was the desire for better accommodation which led to her deciding that what was needed was a Ladies' Club. Getting to and from venues in a wheelchair would have been difficult, and Connie probably stipulated that whatever location was chosen must have easy access. She had probably visited at least one men's club on some special occasion when women were permitted to do so, and was therefore well aware that men were provided with comfortable premises and helpful staff on hand. The fact that women had no such equivalent caused her to feel resentment, and this forced her to reflect. So, within a few months she had got her teeth into a new idea.

This is a speech from Frank Hatt's play, when Constance is being spoken to by Annie, her mother. It conveys Annie's confidence in her daughter:

*"I can't pronounce on the quality of your writing. But your work, your work is more than your writing. And I know that what you can do better than anybody else is to bring people together and show them what they've got inside their hearts and souls and what they can make of themselves."*

*23*

# More About Birmingham

In 1900 Birmingham's wealth, founded on industry and manufacturing and aided by the railways (which were in use in the mid-1850s), was evidenced by splendid civic buildings, fine statues and parks and gardens, though the problem of open sewers and zymotic diseases such as diphtheria or whooping cough, was still prevalent. The view across the town (it would not become a city until 1889) was topped by church spires and chimneys. These were testaments to hard manual work, to ambition, and to low wages. It was Morris's impressive skills, optimistic attitudes and his hopes and fears for society that enabled him to do so much so well for so long.

It is interesting to note that Birmingham had also established a thriving trade in arms – guns, knives and shackles. Bizarrely, the most prolific producer had been the Quaker Samuel Galton (1752-1832) one of whose sons continued to carry on slave trading, which not surprisingly led to a rift between the family and local Quakers.

Charles Dickens in *Pickwick Papers*, revealed his familiarity with poverty, and some of his characters visited plenty of areas that neither Connie or Max were likely to explore.

Despite his attention to artistic affairs and to becoming "a real artist" it is evident that Max was a practical man, very familiar with tools and materials, well able to alter and improve the accommodation – for example, he increased the amount of light in their studio, and did carpentry jobs.

Though he might have visited the town on occasion Max was unlikely to have known Birmingham well. The population in around 1850 was approximately 250,000, many living in unhealthy and squalid accommodation known as back to back "courts". Max's life must have been entirely different from those who occupied such courts.

24

# How Did David and Max Meet?

Having found the letters from my father to Max, I was obviously keen to study them and discover more about the unexpected connection. I wanted to know where, when and why did it start?

David's and Max's lives began to converge from very different and distant starting points at birth. As well as being separated by distance: Canbelego in New South Wales and Ringwood in Hampshire, England, their births were separated by time. Max was born in 1881, and David in 1905. So how was it that they met and became close friends?

No one knows, but my very straightforward suggestion is that they met either while on holiday, probably in Cornwall which, on occasion, they visited at the same time, or perhaps at some meeting or event about an important contemporary subject they were both interested in. I can imagine them chatting over a cup of tea about a presentation they had just heard, and being pleased that they had found someone whose opinions and ideas they shared.

But this may not be correct. For a start, if such an event took place, who knows where and when it took place? Moreover, though I knew that David often attended such events, I cannot be sure that Max did, even if he was keen on the things David was keen on. After all, he was first and foremost a painter, not a sociologist or planner or engineer for the future. And, as far as is known, David could hardly be described as someone passionate about art as Max was.

Another suggestion as to how they met may have come about because my father used to enjoy reaching out to complete strangers with friendly words. Some of those reachings-out bore fruit in that they led to close friendships like the one that the letters show existed between Max and David. Our family was enriched by several new people my father introduced us to, and I describe here two separate occasions which are both family legends.

But first, I found this Celtic Rune of hospitality amongst my father's letters. It mentions a "trinne" which seems to be a Scottish good spirit:

*I saw a stranger yestreen*
*I put food in the eating place*
*Drink in the drinking place*
*Music in the music place*
*In the sacred name of the Trinne.*

*He blessed myself and my home*
*My cattle and my dear ones*
*And the lark said in her song*
*Often, often, often*
*Goes the Christ in the stranger's guise.*

This simple rune seems both to endorse the value of creating chance meetings and to recognise my father's pleasure in doing so.

My father's move to Sheffield in around 1933 had one vitally important feature: he met Phyllis Rose Carr, a professional teacher of ballroom dancing. Despite "The World's Champion Ballroom Dancer" (Victor Silvester) writing *"Miss Phyllis Carr has been under my tuition from time to time. Not only is she a first class exponent of Ballroom Dancing, her technical knowledge and teaching ability being of the highest standard"* David remained uninterested in quicksteps and foxtrots. Though recommended by his employer to learn to dance (for social and business purposes) he wooed Phyllis sitting cross-legged on the studio floor and reading poetry to her.

In 1934 *The Sheffield Daily Telegraph* carried this a small notice:

*"Williamson – Carr.*

*At Christchurch, Lancaster Gate, a Sheffield exponent of ballroom dancing, who is the daughter of the late Mr Marcus Carr, and of Mrs Carr, of Sheffield, was married to Mr David Blair Williamson, B.Sc, son of the late Mr and Mrs William Duncan Williamson, of Greenock."*

They lived first in London, but then bought and moved into a house in a green suburb in Walton-on-Thames in Surrey. They had two sons: Gordon Ridpath (born in 1936) and Roger David Stuart (1938).

Here are two specific and true instances of the sort of thing that David did, and what it led to. The first has nothing to do with Max. Nevertheless, it is relevant.

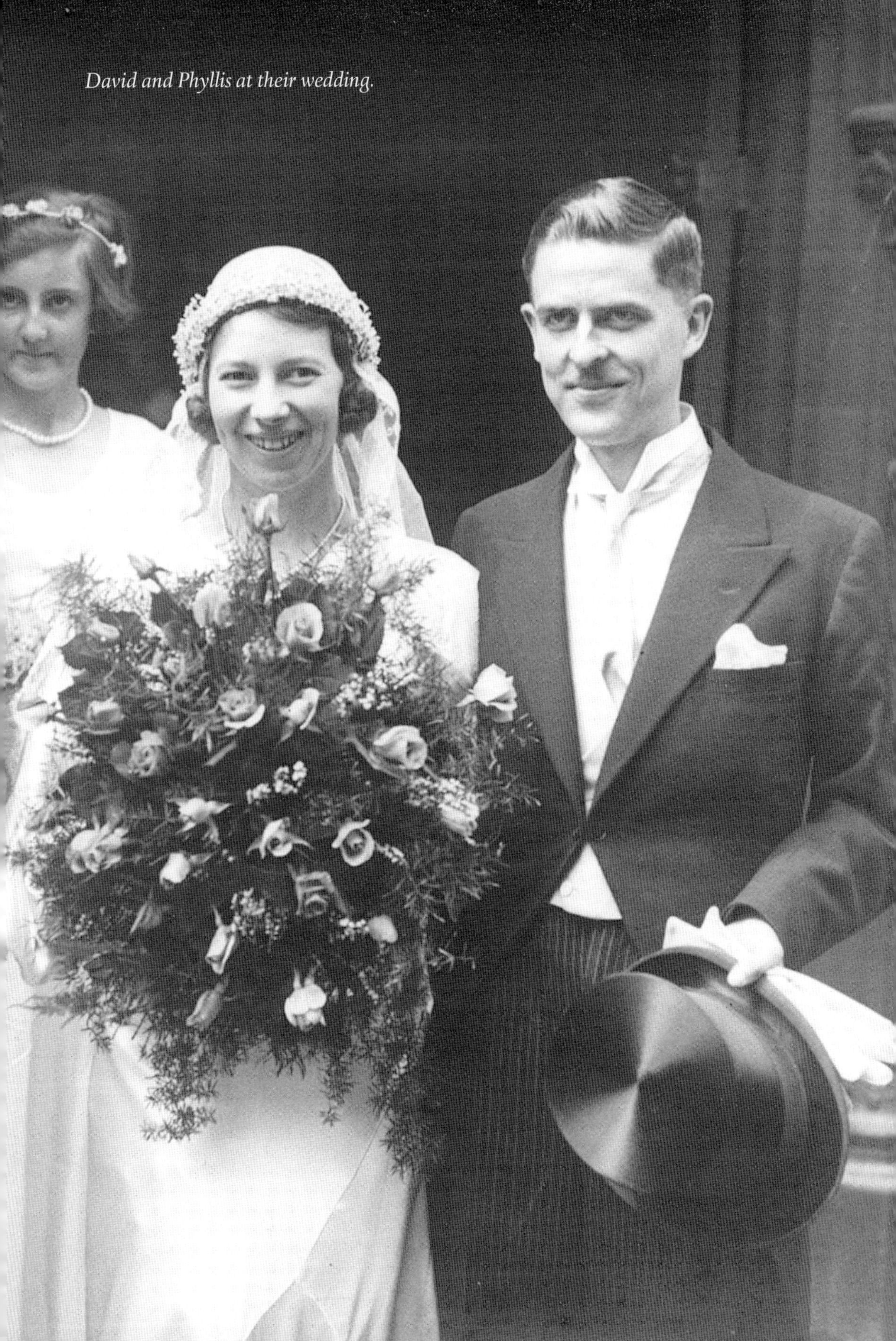

David and Phyllis at their wedding.

**Walter D.**

It was around 1936 when David, strolling through Trafalgar Square on a lovely day not long before WW2 started, noticed a young man in lederhosen. In his usual hospitable manner my father greeted him. It turned out that he was a student from Linz in Austria, named Walter D. The two got into conversation and the meeting ended with David inviting Walter to visit his home in Walton and meet Phyllis and the baby. The invitation was accepted and enjoyed, and though the men never met again, this initial contact led to an important friendship which survived the war and lasted for ten years, thanks partly to the Red Cross who passed on letters and parcels of food.

A parcel my parents sent to Austria on October 31st 1947 enclosed:

1lb sugar
¾ lbs tea
1 lb jam
2 tins sardines
1 lb chocolate
Soap.

This extract is from a letter my father wrote to Walter D. on June 24th.

*"I was very glad to have you letter of 4th April and to know that you are well. Also thankyou for the photograph. You look very well in your greatcoat uniform. I feel I should no longer address you as 'Walter' but as Herr Captain or something of that sort. However I reckon I'll stick to Walter and if you wish you can address me 'David' to make things equal! (Grammar above: 'I'll reckon I'll stick to Walter' is part idiom, part slang and means 'I think I'll continue to use the word Walter'."*

This valuable friendship which linked the Williamsons with an Austrian family stretched over two generations, and still continues, even though time and events have weakened it. But, even if only through Christmas cards and this book, it exists. Another indication of my parents' generosity was that on at least one of the last wartime Christmas Days David invited several German prisoners-of-war to our house for the day. At the time the soldiers were billeted at a local scheme which promoted reconciliation. Over the years, Walter D. and his wife, my brothers and I, and three of Walter D's children, and mothers of both families, have all visited each other's home.

**Brownie S.**

Another legend originated a few days after I was born in August 1943, when my father was worrying about the fact that my mother had no one to help her with me and the two boys. It must have been the school holidays so Gordon and Roger would not have been at school, but bouncing around the house and garden. At that time my father worked in London and was unavailable to look after the children. Not yet having made local friends, and not having relations, my parents had no one to ask for help, and probably very little money to pay someone.

But while on a train near London, David got into conversation with a passenger. She was a complete stranger, a woman named Brownie. She was rather younger than my parents. Brownie and David talked for a while and my father explained his situation. Brownie heard David's anxiety, and then he leaned forward and stretched his hand out across the carriage and grasped Brownie's, saying urgently, "I want *you* to look after them."

And so she did. It was agreed that she should stay at our house and help my mother. I don't know how long she stayed, but it must have been for at least a couple of weeks. And why was she away from her home? I doubt if any money changed hands. Brownie was welcomed and treated as the blessing she was, and so another strong friendship had begun. It continued for decades until her death soon after her 100th birthday. Today her son is still in touch with my brother Roger.

Brownie lived in Polperro, a delightful fishing village in Cornwall and for several years after the war our family went there for our summer holidays, full of excitement about the long train journey, the thought of the sea and of seeing Brownie. The first house we stayed at was *Cliff End*. It had a stunning view of the harbour, the beach and the surrounding cliffs. We were always made very welcome there and later at her other house which was named *The House on the Rocks*.

Polperro was also known to Max because his cousin, Stuart Armfield, lived there. He too was an artist, and he and Max were close. Given the fact that in the late 1940s Cornwall had not yet seen many tourists, it seems quite likely that Stuart and Max, because of their shared interest in painting, could have met my father there just after the end of the war (the watercolour my father had painted in Polperro is dated 1946). Or perhaps David, out for a stroll, just started up a conversation with Max, a man he did not know, and who happened to be working at an easel, sketching the view.

David often drew little pictures on letters or small, homemade cards (rather as Joseph Armfield did) but his watercolour seems to be done on a page torn from a sketch book. His mother, Annie, would have been interested in his painting, but she had died in 1930.

Though these accounts have been about David, rather than about Max, I feel confident that both men were generous spirits who would have made the most of any positive contact, irrespective of who initiated it. David could hardly resist opening a conversation with someone who looked and sounded interesting, and Max, though naturally more shy and perhaps even cautious, would probably have been pleased on being approached by someone he did not know but liked the look of. Consequently, I think he would have reciprocated in like manner.

Of course, even though I know roughly *when* Max and David met, and quite possibly *where* they met, I am unlikely ever to know the precise circumstances of their initial meeting.

# David's Activities and Interests in the War Years

My father's Christian faith was strong. Somehow and somewhere he met Quakers, and began to attend meetings. After several years of attendance, soon after 1940, he became a member of the Society of Friends at Esher meeting, not far from our home.

As a conscientious objector he was not obliged to fight, but he worked as a night time firewatcher.

Perhaps he was fire watching in central London while Max was painting in Chelsea. In 1942 Max completed a portrait of his niece Diana and she wrote about her experience:

*"I enjoyed my several sittings for this portrait. Maxwell was living in Glebe Place off the King's Road Chelsea and once through the door it was a Maxwell interior: a mixture of primitive arrangements and interesting objects, books and pictures. The sittings were largely taken up with drawing, so I didn't see the painting in progress. I had been doing war-time work in a smoke-float factory and the powder had turned my hair into Venetian gold. Maxwell was enamoured of this and suggested that I dressed to it with my gilt necklace and the rather sumptuous jacket which he provided. The portfolio was there to represent my future as a designer. We talked of many things, and every now and then he followed one of his rather abstruse comments with 'I don't suppose you are yet ready for that'. I was mollified by the word 'yet'. He gave me tea in exquisite mended porcelain and had always made for me a plateful of rather heavy biscuit-like cakes which were quite delicious."*

In 1943 and right up until 1948, David was particularly interested in Town and Country Planning. He had various responsibilities in different committees planning for new telecommunications, patterns of work, and ways of living. There is no mistaking the warmth of the testimonials and the appreciation his contribution brought. He wrote a number of papers and articles, such as one entitled *"New Beginnings and New Towns"*. Another one, *"Nothing Can Separate us"*, was published in April 1949 on the front cover of a Friends publication. He also wrote several short plays.

His work, which I understand earned him very little money, took him away from home and even to other countries. At one point he was a civilian lecturer appointed by the British Council to address British troops in the Ruhr about what post-war Britain might be like.

Meanwhile my mother had taken Gordon and Roger to Aberystwyth in Wales for safety, and she and David wrote numerous letters – all full of love – to each other in the early 1940s. David also drew and sent little sketches and cards to the boys, just as Joseph Armfield had done for Max.

But my father was experiencing periods of serious illness. He suffered for much of his adult life with inflammation of the bowel which required him to spend many weeks in hospital.

This illness interrupted not only his career in electrical engineering and his strong interests or, rather, his *passions* about initiatives designed to promote international peace and citizenship, but, obviously it also interrupted his ability to earn a regular salary to support his wife and now three children.

My parents had plans for their children's education. They wanted them to go to a Quaker school, and the school they liked was Sidcot in Somerset. David was keen to find a job in the country, but it is hard to know why he settled on Sidcot, almost halfway across England. Had he been there? Had someone recommended it? However, it was a dream, for he had no job, little money and was ill.

Whatever the situation was, this gentle poem written in December 1948 suggests that he knew the Mendip hills, and longed to settle down in the peace of the countryside:

SIDCOT

*Here in these hollow hills*
*I hoped to dwell,*
*Ringed all about by Sandford and Callow*
*And the ridge of Wavering.*

*Here I could live,*
*Nor be distraught with daily trains,*
*Long journeys*
*And all the jangling miseries of cities.*

*Here see my children grow,*
*Watch the warm sunshine*

*And the western rain suffuse their cheeks*
*With happiness and health.*

*Here would I plant my orchard*
*Row on row of Laxtons, Blenheims*
*And the subtle-flavoured Cox*
*To ripen in the mellow autumn sun.*

*Here talk with friends,*
*Know men, and learn the burden*
*Of the ways of Somerset.*
*Here would I seek for peace*

*And sweet tranquillity*
*As recompense for*
*all the wandering days*
*That I have spent*

*Here in the hollow hills I hoped to live*
*– and die.*

David adored my mother Phyllis whom he often called by her middle name Rose, and he adored his children. On an undated Sunday he began a letter thus:

*"Darling Rose, sweetest and belovedest of wives, mother of sons, sunshine in winter, flower of the Thames valley (and a number of other things into which there is no need to go at the moment).*
*If you are as happy as I am you'll be doing very well. But it cannot be, for I am the happiest mortal on earth."*

And on Feb 16th 1942, after seeing my father in hospital, my mother wrote to her:

*"very darling David: I felt I loved you more than ever. Do take care of yourself, it matters more than anything. I wish I could be looking after you."*

On March 15th of an unknown year my father wrote from his ward on the third floor of the Tropical Hospital, *"I have a tremendous feeling that it's all going to be alright."*
    One day he made a joke about his weight:

*"On the Sunday weigh-in Heavyweight Williamson turned the scales at 9 stone and 1 and a half lb. 3 and a half lbs up on last week. So that's good."*

For medical reasons, I presume, David seemed to move often between hospitals as the years passed. His addresses included St Peter's Hospital in Chertsey, Stratford (on Avon?) Cottage Hospital and Queen Mary Nursing Home, Edinburgh. Both he and my mother wrote about his illness in their letters.

And, despite his illness continuing to trouble him, he and Walter D, with whom he had exchanged at least one letter during the war, recontacted each other and renewed their special and mutually beneficial friendship. David was enthusiastic to tell Walter D. about what he was doing. He wrote:

*"I have been away from home a great deal – in Scotland, Wales and all parts of England, lecturing to all parts of England to all kinds of voluntary groups, Rotary Clubs, Women's Institutes, Youth Groups as well as on the British Commonwealth of free nations. It has been a most interesting experience."*

Letters mattered greatly during the war but David, ill and probably with other correspondence to deal with, made sure he did not forget to write an important letter to his godson who was born in June 1942.

# More About Max and His Fellow Students

Amongst the people Max met at college Arthur Gaskin was a user of tempera and an illustrator of woodcuts for William Morris's Kelmscott Press. He was promoted to a lectureship while he was still a student. Like Max, he too benefitted from the company of his friend Joseph Southall. He married Georgina, known as Georgie, another art student. They started producing jewellery and in 1903 Arthur Gaskin became head of a school for jewellers and Silversmiths. Despite this Max says little about him in his essay *"My Approach to Art"*.

Max's essay is informative, fluent and thoughtful. In it he outlines his personal history and places himself within his time. When he arrived at Birmingham the Arts and Crafts Movement made famous by William Morris and John Ruskin was beginning to fade. But Max found much beauty in its painting and decoration which he could benefit from and contribute to. He was well aware he was "under the pre-Raphaelite spell".

The Movement was partly driven by Socialists, but although Max had grown up in a liberal and intelligent milieu, he could not be described as political. His focus was almost entirely directed to whatever painting or drawing was flat on the table or up on the easel in front of him. Painting came first, almost every time. In essence, his creative approach was solidly founded on ceremony and ritual, and he never relied on emotion to inform his work.

So involved was he with whatever artistic project was in hand, that he made little comment about his fellow students or, indeed, about Birmingham itself: not its buildings, nor its people nor its busy-ness. The fact that it was one of the major centres of the Arts and Crafts Movement was significant, but this did not mean that it impressed Max, for he wrote:

*"Apart from invaluable benefit from guidance and advice from such masters as Henry Payne, Arthur Gaskin, Norman Wilkinson and Joseph Southall, I really taught myself, as must any one who hopes to do individual work… I detested the Life Class, and rarely attended it: I refused to learn perspective or anatomy as they bored me, and generally, I could not have been a worse student."*

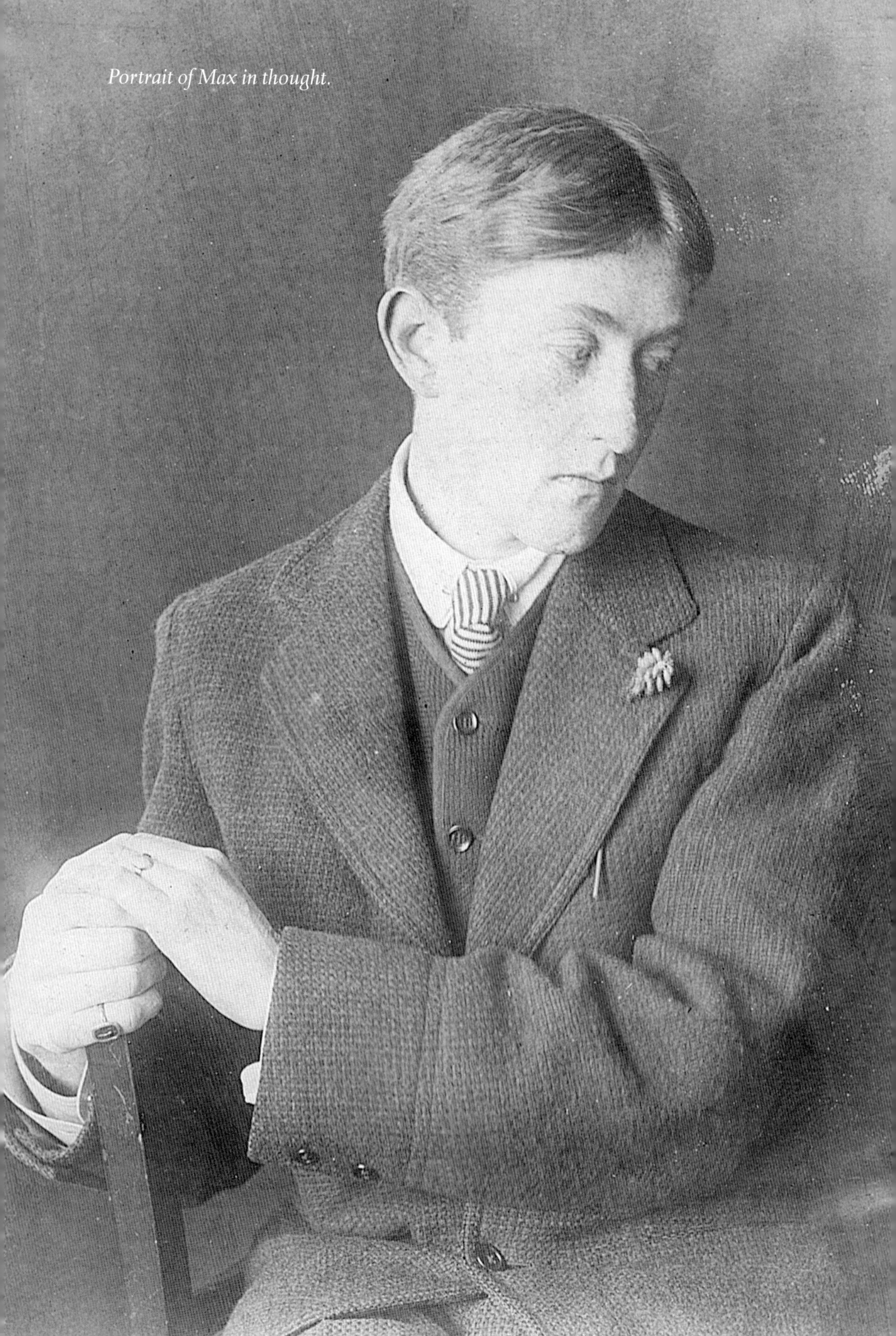
Portrait of Max in thought.

And another – more positive – clue to how he felt about his college in this extract from *Tempera Painting Today (40)*:

> *"I remember very well my inward rage when, after dealing very kindly with my sugary attempts in purple and pink at the age of nineteen, my teacher suggested that I should do well to copy some Italian primitives. I thought them still, wooden and perfectly hideous in every particular. But, fortunately, for only a few hours. …*
> *… One might as well sit on a tree branch and determinedly saw it off beneath one to escape producing a 'pastiche' as attempt to produce serious work without first laboriously studying and copying the previous masters…"*

Surprisingly, and rather disappointingly, Max is sparing in what he writes about Joseph Southall. This was the man who was a key influence on Max, despite not actually being a member of the School's staff. He was particularly helpful in that he taught Max about tempera. Southall was a member of the Society of Friends.

# Painting in Tempera

Max came to prefer using tempera to any other paint medium. It is, in essence, a creamy liquid made of glue, coloured pigments, water and a very small amount of (raw) egg yolk. Its beauty for the artist is first and foremost its luminosity. Important too is the fact that it adheres and dries fast. Moreover, it is part of a long tradition that continues to have visual resonance. The picture on the dust jacket of Max's book *Tempera Painting Today* (dedicated to Stuart Armfield) features what looks like half a hard-boiled egg being bitten – or perhaps eaten – by two fierce dragon-like creatures, the words "oil" and "water" and two paint brushes.

These are odd images unless one knows what they mean, and of course Max did nothing without a sound reason. So, the cover is a visual statement of the book's three-worded title and even of its contents. In tempera painting there must be liquid egg yolk (though that in the picture looks solid, as does the white of the egg). Nevertheless, the egg is more than just *in* the centre, it *is* the centre. Eggs represent new life, unhatched potential, and the circle of life. In the east, dragons symbolise power and wealth. Elsewhere, they signify chaos.

The book's text would seem to promote the use of tempera to all artists, but Max denied that his purpose was to get everyone to use it: he just wanted students and painters to know that they would benefit from knowing more about it.

This activity was a ritual for Max, requiring attendance, vigilance, even mysticism. Max is likely to have painted every day because that was his life's purpose. It was rare for anything to take precedence unless other plans had already been agreed on.

Egg tempera is a medium which required different materials, tools and methods of application from those needed by painters who preferred conventional water-colours, oils, pastels, charcoal and so on. Tempera's highly sought after qualities have attracted artists for centuries, from before the Greeks and Romans, right up to and beyond the Italian Renaissance today.

Max, focused yet relaxed, would embark on his tempera work in an unhurried, even solemn mood. He would prepare for the session with care. First he selected a board to paint on. Though he also painted on card, canvas and even paper, his preference when using tempera was almost always board. Earlier in the day, or even the day before, he would have made a solution of distemper pigment (an ancient type of whitewash mixed with rabbit skin glue), mixed it, heated it cautiously and left it over night. He knew it was ready when it stuck his fingers gently together. The first task was to paint one layer of this on the board, but if the solution was not quite right, he may have had to dilute it with a little water and chalk whitening until it was the consistency of single cream. When the board was dry he sanded down each layer, trying to make the board as smooth as possible. He then repeated this process *nine* times. The task usually lasted all day, so sometimes he must have devoted entire days to preparing a batch of boards. Finally, he was ready to paint.

Tempera is not a messy type of painting, and, compared to an artist who needs huge canvasses, long handled brushes, buckets of paint and a range of different materials and equipment, Max took up little space in his studio. Once the board was ready, he then had to prepare the colours. He would have needed merely a palette and maybe a palette knife, a small amount of water, an egg yolk and the colour pigments. The pigments, looking wonderful in their little glass containers, have special names such as:

Alizarine crimson
Terre de sienne brulee
Ocre jaune
Titanium white
Coral red
Cobalt turquoise.

He probably bought these at Cornelissen's in London, a treasure trove of art materials founded by colourman Louis Cornelissen in around 1881. The business is now in Great Russell Street.

When Max was ready he would have taken an egg, broken its shell carefully, letting the white slip away from the yolk through his fingers into a sink. Then he would have rinsed the yolk before puncturing its soft sac carefully, urging it into a small container, and taking it to where he was going to use it. Then he would have chosen a small brush because tempera artists tend to paint smaller pictures in small strokes rather than large pictures in large strokes. And he would have begun to apply the paint to the bright white surface.

The subjects of Max's pictures are very varied, as are his techniques, and his essay *My Approach to Art* gives plenty of his thoughts, experiences and reminiscences. For example: the sea, landscapes, the sky, the coast.

And here is an anecdote that Diana Armfield had written which revealed another side to Connie. This incident occurred at a time when Connie's eyesight was deteriorating, and a family discussion was underway about what could be done to help her.

Diana wrote:

*"On one visit to Oak Tree in my teens, Constance suggested that I should live with them for a time, have art tuition from Maxwell and in return read aloud to Constance.*

*The idea filled me with instant alarm, fortunately understood by Gertrude* and the matter was dropped. I have always had a strong regard for Max, however badly he behaved, but Constance I feared from the strength of her character."*

Unfortunately, we do not know what Max thought of the idea. And even more unfortunately we do not know what his bad behaviour consisted of.

---

*  Possibly the housekeeper.

# Connie and the Lyceum

It was about 1902 or 1903 when Connie began to talk more and more about founding a club for women, and the idea seems to have been *hers*, though she had four important friends whom she designated as her "co-ajudtors". These four were Christina Gowans Whyte (a children's author), Elsa Hahn, Violet Alcock and Jessie Trimble (who was American). Not much is known about any of them but I can imagine them being sounding boards for Connie, enabling her to bounce ideas around. Like her, they were members of the Writer's Club in London whose simple and solid aim was to "Advance the cause of letters". But the aims of this yet-to-be founded club, which was gradually being brought alive by young women, was more ambitious. They wanted to provide a comfortable, elegant and creative environment. The club, in short, was to be a place of pleasure, business and interest for women.

Long discussions fuelled the ambitions of Connie and her friends until they had definitively resolved to make it happen. There were a few such clubs in London already, such as the New County Club and the Empress, but none of these provided as much as the one which Connie and her co-ajudtors had in mind.

There was also a shortage of clubs for those who were not considered (and perhaps would not claim) to be middle class, despite holding down (poorly) paid jobs and lodging independently in their own rooms rather than living with their parents. A character in Edith Wharton's *House of Mirth* is on the committee of a charity planning to provide comfortable lodgings, with a reading room and other modest distractions where young women employed in New York's downtown offices might find a home when out of work or in need of rest.

Frances Power Cobbe, a suffragist and anti-vivisectionist, had strong opinions about the proposed club. She asked *"Is it not possible for ladies to possess a Club which will not afford too striking a contrast with the splendours of St James?"* She then commented that whenever the idea was mooted *"the poverty of women, as regards ability to incur any unusual expense, become curiously revealed…"* – that is, women who appeared wealthy and *"lapped in excessive luxury, provided for them by the affection of husbands and fathers actually had no money of their own to expend on such a project and the affectionate husbands and fathers would not,"* she surmised, *"be prepared to give their money towards providing a club for their wives and daughters."*

Such comments spell out the practice whereby even well-off women were not – or still are not – in charge of their own budgets, but have to rely on what men give them.

What Connie and Frances Cobbe and an increasing number of other women hoped for was not complicated. They wanted *"a substantial and dignified milieu where women could meet editors and other employers and discuss matters as men did in professional clubs: above all in surroundings that did not suggest poverty."*

They also wanted the club's members to create and promote sound relationships with women in other countries.

As already depicted, Connie was a forceful woman, and her proposal was an initiative that required her to push plenty of boundaries. There must have been many people around – quite probably women as well as men – who said things such as: *"Whatever will they want next?"* or *"Why would women prefer to be out at a club when they can be at home?"* or *"Great Scott! Things have gone too far!"* Setting up an organisation which was essentially for the advancement of women was – as everyone knew – not going to be straightforward.

Connie proceeded by telling everyone of her plans. Of course she turned to her family, and happily, as always, her parents supported her. Her sister Di did too, but as a committed suffragette she was already involved with various women's organisations. There is little information about Di and Connie's brother Billie (a rather headstrong and likeable young man) and at this stage of his life it is unlikely that he contributed anything other than comments.

As we know, Connie was not as politically radical as Di and seeking franchise for women was not her main goal, but in 1903 her idea of creating a women's club was firming up. Many people (including some men) were interested and keen to see a respectable club like the one Connie envisaged: somewhere where professional and artistic women could hang up their coats and hats, enjoy entertainments, share ideas, eat and drink, rest and even stay overnight. The absence of men had one other benefit. This was not that males were not wanted per se (though there may have been some truth in that), it was rather that women could have their own territory in the same way that men did, and be free of actual or perceived criticism from men as well as having to put up with unwanted male attention. And perhaps they also liked the fact that such a club would be somewhere where men *did not get in the way.*

Connie told her father of her plans, and kept him up to date with her progress – or lack of it. He was more than willing to help her and her four aides. It was decided that Connie should approach the officers of the Writers Club, and float her simple proposal which was that there should be a special section provided for women. She

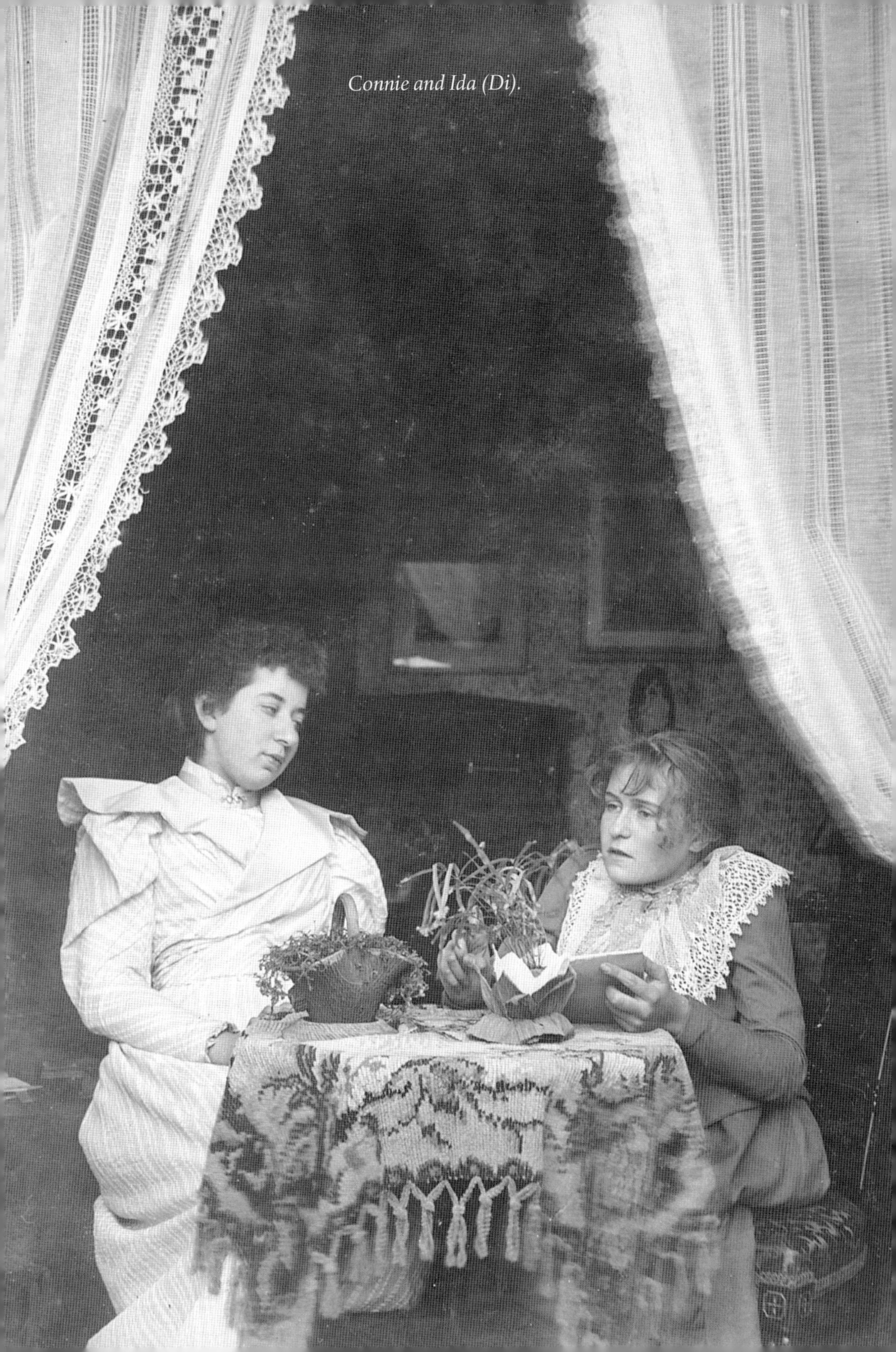

*Connie and Ida (Di).*

voiced her suggestion, and when she was asked, *"And who is to organise this?"* Connie announced that she would do it herself. To her embarrassment and disappointment the whole project was put down and perfunctorily dismissed.

But this set-back did not deter her or her colleagues for long. They began to assemble a Provisional Committee, and sent out sixty notices about the club-to-be. This led to more disappointment because only two people responded. How demoralising. Two? Only two? How could women *not* want a club for themselves? But this setback did not knock Connie's confidence to the ground. She just had to rethink her plans.

She couldn't do much without money. As well as renting or buying premises, the premises of the club – whose existence was still imaginary – would be likely to require at least decorating, altering and furnishing. So she asked her father for money and, easily able to afford to help her, he offered her a substantial sum to start the club off. But before actually giving her the money he made a condition: Connie had to show that she had enough women to make the proposal viable in the long run. He wasn't going to bale her out if she found herself in financial trouble.

William stipulated that the club should have at least one thousand members, each paying a guinea (one pound and one shilling in British currency at the time) per annum. Connie, fired with this new challenge – it should be clear by now that she embraced challenges – resolved to try again. She decided to open the club to women in a range of professions (not just to writers and illustrators, as had been decided earlier) and also – significantly – to some daughters and wives of "distinguished men" known to her socially. This increased the field, albeit creating an uncomfortable – indeed illogical – situation whereby the eligibility for some women to join depended on their relationship to a man. But the strategy worked in business terms and after a renewed campaign to attract members, one thousand women stated that they were keen to join the club whose Provisional Committee was already being appointed. William Smedley honoured his promise and gave Connie £30,000 – a vast sum equivalent to at least three and a half million pounds today – without which the club could not possibly have gone ahead. Connie, determined that women should be independent, must have had some contradictory thoughts and feelings about the fact that the club was only able to come into existence because a man was prepared to fund it. But she couldn't have done it by any other means, so wasn't going to turn the offer down.

One of Connie's books, *Conflict,* was the direct result of her spending time with women who had to earn their own living. Strangely, although she must always have been used to having housekeepers, maids and kitchen staff in her parents' or her friends' various homes, the Writers' Club seems to be one of very few places where she took notice of them and thought about their lives. It seems rather surprising that "women who had to earn their own living" would have attended clubs such as the Writers' Club at all. If they did so, surely Connie must have met them already, so how did she square her conscience when faced with a kitchen worker or seamstress who would certainly not be able to afford the Lyceum's membership fee? One hopes that, at some point while she was thinking about the potential club and its potential members, she could not fail to acknowledge and reflect on the difference between her life and the life of working women. Meeting them surely began to give her a wider concept of women: about what they do and how they do it, and what they and she *could* be and what they and she *could* do.

Of course, Connie was not alone. Many people are well aware of their own contradictions, and of how they justify them. And giving up privilege is difficult.

*29*

# The Lyceum and the Women's Movement

So Connie entered a phase of her life where the plans for the club were usually centre stage for her, but before she became engulfed she found time to squeeze in some more writing. This time she wove herself into some of her early child-like stories which are set in her "Kingdom". She created a world of legend, invented a cast of characters linked to her real-life friends, and featured them in her books. She gave herself the role of "Peter" who, in folk story tradition, is the third son of a miller. His two elder brothers are confident about life because they know they will inherit all of their father's wealth, whereas Peter will have to use his wits to make a living.

But that last point seems to be the only similarity between Peter and Connie herself, because, unlike Peter, she had two options. If she were to remain true to her principles, she would abandon her plans for the club because she would not accept a man's money. The other route was to go ahead using a man's money and do her best to repay it. As we know she accepted her father's incredibly generous contribution. Does this count as "using her wits"? Hardly. But perhaps Peter thought it was.

The putative club was being talked about in the Smedley household at the same time as the suffragettes' demands were beginning to take centre stage in London. Each member of the Smedley family was determined that women should have the vote. The sisters championed the suffragettes in very different ways. Rather than spending her time demonstrating and attending meetings, Di threw herself into her studies and often worked late into the small hours. She became an authority on fatty acids, which came within her field of bio-chemistry, and these activities were part of her important contribution to the Women's Movement. At the same time she was bringing up her two children so her life must have been packed with activity. This can be looked at in two ways. A quick glance suggests that because she was so busy she could not have had any time for herself. But in fact what she did was almost entirely *for* herself, because she was doing precisely what she wanted to do, whether that was carrying out a test in a laboratory, or soothing an upset child or writing a letter. Getting the balance right is difficult and one that, on the whole and even now at the time of writing, more women than men have to struggle to achieve.

Meanwhile, Connie was fully engaged dealing with all that the embryonic club demanded of her: finances, publicity, kitchens, staff, furniture, alterations and so on. Her contribution to the better world was the provision of a place where women could and would be able to thrive as well as men did in their clubs.

It is not known how Mrs Smedley felt about her daughters' participation in direct action, or even her opinion about their low-key involvement at demonstrations and meetings. But we can be certain that, even if anxious about some public disorder in London, she and William would have been proud at what Connie and Di were doing.

So, equipped with hope, £30,000 and a sense of urgency Connie and her co-mates searched for and found prestigious (and presumably extremely expensive) premises at 128 Piccadilly in London. As well as being both comfortable and having pleasant surroundings the property was convenient and central. Plans for drawing rooms, dining rooms, bathrooms – even a library and an art gallery – were being made, and as the women's ambition grew, they realised that they had reached the point when they needed the oxygen of publicity. After all, their club had not even got a name.

It was Jessie Trimble who thought up the name: *International Lyceum Club for Women Artists and Writers*. The word "Lyceum" had an appealing classical ring about it, entirely appropriate for a club whose aims were and continue to be to promote women's emancipation and world peace. Some aims! One can imagine the excitement as more women wanted to join and did so, as the premises were altered to what was needed, and as journalists turned up looking for a story.

Though the club had Connie for its secretary it urgently needed a figurehead. The names of numerous women were considered, discussed and rejected.

Who could do the job? Who? It had to be a feminist, someone already well-known, someone who was already supporting the Lyceum's raison d'être.

And then Lady Frances Balfour was suggested. It was immediately felt that she would be very suitable. Born in 1858, she was a Scot, the sister-in-law of J. J. Balfour (the then prime minister) a liberal and an aristocrat. A non-violent suffragist, she held various offices such as the Presidencies of both the "National Society for Woman's Suffrage", and the "London Society for Woman's Suffrage". When first approached by Connie and her chief collaborators, she declined to take on yet another responsibility. However, after more discussion she changed her mind.

She proved to be an excellent and enthusiastic choice. She met all the criteria that Connie and her co-adjutors had decided their figurehead needed to meet. Even better, she agreed to be the club's figurehead for fifteen years, thus adding stability.

It is interesting to note that she had had problems with a hip joint from infancy. This was always painful and caused her to limp, but both she and Connie got on with life despite their disabilities and neither complained about the impact these surely must have had on them. Nevertheless, it seems likely that their similar situation added a special, strong (and probably unmentioned) dimension to their relationship.

Then began the business of actually creating a programme of talks and recitals and discussions. Approaches had to be made to possible speakers or musicians. Advertisements had to be distributed or displayed. A timetable and diary had to be worked out. Refreshments had to be provided. Simultaneously maids, cooks, doormen and cleaners had to be appointed. One of Connie's concerns was that the furnishings of the club should be elegant, the meals good, the accommodation comfortable. She also stressed that there should be no whiff of poverty. Indeed, her determination that no one should find the club to lack quality and status was always in her mind. Achieving the standard she wanted meant spending money, and luckily for her, money was available.

*The present day logo of The International Association of Lyceum Clubs.*

# The Lyceum Opens

The club opened its doors in June 1904 to admit its first members. They must have been both curious and pleased to be there. For some, the first meeting they attended may have been the one that convinced them that the Lyceum was going to be A Good Thing. Others may have taken longer to realise what a relaxed and pleasant evening could be passed there. Soon, many of them would have come to value what was on offer at the Lyceum, to enjoy the company of others and to encourage their like-minded friends to join.

Connie was careful to hold on to the Lyceum's principles and purpose and not let it degenerate into a mere social club. The committee established sub-committees each with its own agenda, and these produced Club Bulletins. An afternoon at the club might include lunch, a talk, a practical demonstration of, for example, weaving. Or perhaps a discussion in French. Outings to famous places were arranged, and going to films together was also popular.

As news of the club spread, expressions of interest began to be voiced from other countries. Although Connie had probably been to the continent occasionally, there is nothing to suggest that she had done so often or for substantial periods. However, growing up as she did, in the Smedley household, she was used to meeting people from other countries.

Therefore, when people overseas heard about the Lyceum, she took the opportunity to involve them and encourage them to set up Lyceum clubs in their own countries. Increased internationalism was one of the principles on which the Lyceum club was founded, so Connie was obviously going to promote it and pacifism where she could. One of her initiatives to interest another country was when, in 1905, the Lyceum hosted an Anglo-German dinner. This event:

*"attracted a formidable list of guests which included the Earl and Countess of Aberdeen, the entire diplomatic staff of the German Embassy, the Lord Mayor of London and the editors of two of the more level-headed organs of British public opinion: George Prothero from the Quarterly Review and Austin Harrison from the Observer. Speeches given by the German Ambassador, Count Metternich, Lord Aberdeen and Smedley herself, focused on the urgent need – in Prothero's*

*words – for 'those who write and who address great masses of persons, to do all they can to quench the flame of enmity.' Constance Smedley herself pleaded that night for 'the English to remember that Germany was not merely a commercial nation, but the land of art and literature, of Beethoven and Bach, of Handel and Wagner, Strauss and Schubert that is the Germany we love'."*

But in 1918 things were rather different when a Mrs Sheepshanks read out a letter at a Lyceum dinner, causing The Executive Committee of the Lyceum Club to pass a resolution stating that *"the reading of this letter from an enemy alien was a deliberate insult to British women present at the dinner".* Mrs Sheepshanks was banned from future admission to the Club.

Italy showed interest too, as did Amsterdam and Berlin. And in 1908 Florence had its own Lyceum club. The name of the first Italian President was Beatrice Pandolfini dei Principi. She was a land owner and aristocrat who might, today, be surprised to find that the family estate is occupied by the Italian Academy of Cuisine Pandolfini.

Frances Balfour is a less imposing name, and her life in the rather Spartan-looking Whittinghame Tower in Scotland was perhaps more modest that that of her Italian counterpart, but her work with suffragettes meant she was held in high regard. It should be emphasised that Connie, unashamedly, wanted members of the upper classes to join the club because they added prestige, interest and all-important contacts she could 'grow' and build into her networks.

But things were certainly not always grandiose or formal. When Connie travelled to another German city, Hamburg, she found that the Women's Club there stated that *"according to article 7, 'members' guests (including men) may use the powder rooms free of charge."* On this point it seems that the Women's Club Hamburg was a step ahead of its London counterpart.

But of course clubs did not *always* deliver good events and speakers, and the efforts of the various committees were not always appreciated, as these comments evidence:

*"Somerville and Ross (an Anglo-Irish writing team) attended an Irish evening at the Lyceum in 1906 at which Standish O'Grady (Irish novelist and writer) was chief guest. They thought it a pity, after suffering 'his very long and wandering and dreary speech that he had left a rest cure in order to make it.' Worse followed, for there was 'a horrid youth who spoke as if his mouth was full of fishbones', a Miss Hull who sermonised on her part in the Gaelic revival 'in a thin mouselike squeak' and a mad woman from Australia. And then Miss Coleman Smith chanted Yeats' poetry. Thoroughly browned off, Somerville and Ross decided to be guests of honour at the St Patrick's day dinner to be held at the Lyceum in 1907."*

# Max in France

In 1902, after three successful and productive years at the Birmingham School of Art, Max visited France. It was probably but not necessarily his first time out of England, but whether it was or not the visit must have astonished, excited and delighted him. Regrettably there is lack of clarity about whom he travelled with. Although he writes using the first person, it definitely feels as if he is with someone else. In his work he does not refer to or address this unnamed companion, though he acknowledges that he had gone at the instigation of Gaskin *"who thought I was now ready to gain from the experience"*. Or, it could well have been Southall.

Both these two, Gaskin and Southall, when young men in the 1880s, had benefitted greatly by making several (separate) long journeys on the continent.

And now Max did so too, and he wrote *"All in all this visit established and made secure all that I had learned at Birmingham"*. So, yet again, Max took advantage of this opportunity to get the maximum benefit from the visit, but despite feeling that he was making progress he expressed his frustration at his inability to know *why* he liked certain aspects and achievements of his work, and that was the question which pushed him to explore, while in France, what lay underneath the surface of art.

Some weeks or months later, after this happy and educational foray, it is likely that he went back to Ringwood for a while to his family. He had decided to move to Paris to study at the Académie de la Grande Chaumière: so he was facing another beginning.

Max must have been one of the *Académie*'s very first students, because a plaque on the main building announcing the foundation of the school gives that date as 1904. The school was started by two women, one Swiss and one Russian. One of them refused to teach the traditional strict rules of painting that were de rigeur at the *École de Beaux Arts*. Indeed, it was stated that the Académie *"fut, en quelque sorte un lieu de résistance et de création pure"*, meaning that it was, in some way, a place of resistance and of pure creation.

The school was headed up by a Catalan artist, Claudio Castelucho. It had a *"vaste atelier"* in which students could *"practiquer leur art intemporel"*. Another artist voiced, *"Académie de la Grande Chaumière est la seule institution qui, au debout du siècle ait ouvert la voie d'art"*. The school was best known for its life drawing and naked models where artists worked in *"croquis, fusain, dessin et peintre à huile"* (pencil, charcoal, drawing and oil paints). Later on, numerous art students studied there, including Giacometti, Poliakof, Miro and Modigliani.

*Translation:*
*The school was headed up by a Catalan artist, Claudio Castelucho. It was a large studio in which students could practise their timeless art. Another artist stated that "The school of the Big Cottage" was the only institution which, at the beginning of the century, had opened the way for art. The school was best known for its life drawings and naked models where artists worked in pencil, charcoal, drawing and oil paints. At the art school Max met Gustave Courtois (later to become a highly respected sculptor) and René Menard. He also studied with Gaston Lachaise, and shared a studio with Keith Henderson, who would become a war artist, and Norman Wilkinson, who would become the inventor of dazzle painting designed to protect ships in WW1.*

Perhaps Max focussed entirely on painting, but let us hope that there were at least some occasions when he explored Paris. What did he do and see and feel there? Surely he would not have been able to ignore the cornucopia of contemporary architecture which included the Ceramic Hotel, the Viaduc d'Austerlitz, the Grand Palais, the Petit Palais and the Gare du Lyon? And did he go to see work by Matisse or Picasso? If so, what did he think of it? An artist he particularly admired was Giovanni Segantini, an Italian landscape painter.

Did he ever enjoy the haute cuisine of, say, the special Train Bleu Restaurant, or stand on the trottoirs roulants and be conveyed along the pavement? Or see the Eiffel Tower in its special exhibition coat of yellow paint? Things were changing fast: horse drawn fiacres were gradually being replaced by motor cars; the Metro was conveying its first passengers. And – perhaps of no interest to Max at all, but nevertheless extremely important to many French people – the winner of the first Tour de France was stripped of his title in 1903, on being accused of cheating.

Max's decision to study in France coincided with the signing of the Entente Cordiale, a series of agreements made in 1904 with the aim of improving Anglo-French relations. The Entente achieved its goal but there is little to suggest that it made Max any more interest in politics. However, at least he was making his own contribution by living in and getting to know France for a while.

He was a diligent worker. Many of his diary entries refer to work in hand, except when something unusual displaced his routine as it did occasionally. For example, when he returned to Ringwood for three weeks he did no painting. Of course he would have been welcomed warmly, and the family must have been extremely interested in and admiring and proud of his paintings. He must have changed a lot in the previous few years and would have looked at his home, his family and Ringwood differently. And his family must have looked differently at him, too, for he had changed from a young and unusual student to a serious artist whose name was just beginning to become known, who had attended an art college abroad, and whose life was opening up. Also, by this time Max probably spoke good French.

As if to emphasise that he was back in England the first painting he completed was of a sight common to Londoners: Oxford Circus underground station, with a train in a tunnel. It was quite unlike his other work: sombre and still.

Max continued to submit his work to galleries, and, in common with numerous other artists he was disappointed and bruised when his work was turned down. But there were people who believed in him. After one rejection he wrote, *"When I got home I found a very encouraging letter from Mr Southall who is 'rigid' with indignation at them for turning out my picture. Feel much better today."*

"Them" must refer to those people selecting paintings for a particular unnamed exhibition. How good of Joseph Southall to take the time to bolster Max's spirits.

But despite the fact some of his work did not gain attention, there was success and excitement too. One special event took place in 1904 when his painting *Faustine* was bought by the French state and exhibited at the Paris Salon. It features a fleshy flashy female figure in a bright red dress. She takes up most of the picture and looks straight at the viewer while a Max-like man at the edge of the picture leans towards her bold shape. *Faustine* was inspired by a long poem by Algernon Swinburne, the poet who was a symbol of decadence. It is said that he wrote about vices such as cannibalism and bestiality, and that he liked to be flogged. But one would not guess that from these first few verses of *Faustine*:

*Lean back, and get some minutes' peace;*
   *Let your head lean*
*Back to the shoulder with its fleece*
   *Of locks, Faustine.*

*The shapely silver shoulder stoops,*
   *Weighed over clean*
*With state of splendid hair that droops*
   *Each side, Faustine.*

> *Let me go over your good gifts*
> *That crown you queen;*
> *A queen whose kingdom ebbs and shifts*
> *Each week, Faustine.*

The French donated Max's painting to the Musée du Luxembourg and it is now in the *Musée d'Orsay*, Paris. This honour marked the first really significant point in Max's career.

*La Académie Colarossi* was another art school in Paris. It had been founded by an Italian sculptor in 1815 and it closed in the 1930s. Max is reported to have attended it, but there is doubt about whether that was so or not, and the facts are no longer available because, unfortunately (for researchers and for Signor Colarossi, at least) Madame Colarossi burned the valuable archives of the institution in retaliation for her husband's philandering.

# Max's Friendships

Max made new friends – though not particularly close ones – when he went to college. He kept well away from noisy groups, but in Birmingham and in France he often went out to concerts and plays. Perhaps he attended these on his own? Certainly, it is clear that he liked intellectual conversations and over his life he met plenty of like-minded people.

He also painted many portraits of people he knew. Over the years he painted his mother, himself (several times), and many more including Keith Henderson, Norman Wilkinson, his sister, Gaston Lachaise, Diana Armfield, MacKnight Kauffer, Alexander Ballard and Gwen Lewis. Most of his portraits were of personal friends.

Max's activities at Sidcot, in Ringwood, in Birmingham and abroad have been described, but what of his private and personal life? There is little to say, other than the fact that most people who knew him or who knew about him state that he was gay.

Had he had "a little flirt" at Sidcot? Had he had boy or girl friends when at the art school in Birmingham? What about while in France?

Is there a clue in a painting he completed while he was a student, in 1902? Entitled *Oh Willo! Willo! Willo!* it is essentially based on an old song about lost love. What did Max know about lost love when he was 20 or 21? Had he by then had any, or many, relationships, including sexual ones? With men or women? Given his education and home background that seems unlikely. While we know he strongly admired a Miss Lewis and perhaps other women when he was in Birmingham, we do not know if he became close to anyone. Virtually nothing is known of his intimate personal life. Max did not write about his sexuality, and it seems that no one else did either, so we are left looking, unsuccessfully, for snips of comments from people who met him.

But there was one comment about the painter Duncan Grant, who was said to have had what was called "a mild flirtation" with the "eccentric" Maxwell Armfield. Emmanuel Cooper (who was gay, a ceramicist, and an art critic) described the scene when Max met Grant in the National Gallery.

On a day in 1903 or 1904, Duncan Grant was copying the angels in Piero della Francesca's *Nativity* when he was noticed by Max. Grant must have become aware of the slim young artist working in the same gallery, and of the increasing number of glances that were coming his way. So impressed was Max by Grant's good looks that he introduced himself and for a brief time the two were lovers. But Grant found the precise, slightly old-fashioned attitudes of Max did not suit his own expansive mood and they soon drifted apart. It is interesting that Max, though the younger of the two, seemed to be the more conservative – at least in Grant's eyes.

So, given that there is no evidence to the contrary, it seems as if at this period of his life (his early twenties) Max was gay or bi-sexual. He would not have been open about it because for a man to have sexual relationships with a man (or a woman with a woman) was socially unacceptable to many, and homosexual acts even between consenting men over 21, were still illegal until the 1967 Sexual Offence Act.

Looking briefly to 1906 when Max was again returning to England, he decided to call himself Evelyn Grant-Stuart. That new name (which may have been chosen because of his friendship with Duncan Grant) appeared in a catalogue published for an exhibition he was to hold with Gaston Lachaise. The reason for this new name was that Max was becoming interested in astrology and he sometimes chose to use other names for particular pieces of work he created under certain astrological circumstances. He did not abandon his given name or his monogram although later still he used a variety of other names as a cover for his writings about the occult. This may have been to protect him in the art world, whose members might have criticised his new interests and so restricted him.

After his adventures abroad, Max might have wanted to settle for a while, and just enjoy being at home. Or perhaps his family put pressure on him to spend time with them. Either way, by this point it might well have been the case that Ringwood was now too small for him. There would have been little privacy and no room to grow.

So, where next? And what next?

Max would have wanted to consider re-establishing himself in London. But would he do that on his own? We know that his father was still paying him because a note in his (Max's) journal, dated October 5th 1914, states his decision to give up that allowance. Before he felt confident enough to be financially independent, one presumes he must have had some money coming in, and at least a couple of exhibitions in sight.

Diana Armfield was well aware of Max's frequent requests for money to his brother, Harold, and said that although he was given money, he did not understand financial arrangements and often complained and questioned why he could not have more (as he grew older Max's father must have given the responsibility for looking after the family's wealth to Max's younger brother Harold. It was probably a wise move).

# Connie Appears

Max needed to find somewhere to live, and he moved many times in his life, renting, buying and selling, though his reason for doing so was not always clear. However, one significant move was to Kelmscott, at Acocks Green near Birmingham. William Morris of the Arts and Crafts had lived and had his Press there from 1860-1865. Morris, introduced in an earlier chapter, was an erratic, unique and nervous man. He was also an achiever in many fields, and the author of the classic *News from Nowhere* which describes a better world and promotes social good and freedom from oppression. His socialist maxim was *Fellowship is Life.*

At this point, around 1904 or 1905, Max had not yet made any mention of Connie in his journal. But now she appeared, probably at Kelmscott.

It is not known precisely how and when the couple met but Max gives a very personal account of his feelings about Connie in his journal. This is what he wrote about her on October 12th 1907:

*"Have been away at Lulworth Cove all summer doing water-colours that are by far the best things I have ever done ... I am happier than before. Since the last entry I have met and become one of the nearest friends of Constance Smedley. She is too wonderful to describe our friendship, some friendship is too wonderful to last very long but although that my love be so it is worth it over and over again. She has helped me as no-one else except Gwen ever has and I am glad to think that I have sometimes helped her."*

This is Max's first reference to Gwen since his Birmingham days. We know nothing about her unless she is a violinist from Wales of the same name. Or perhaps she was a student? But, whoever she was, she was important to Max, not least because he painted a portrait of her.

Max's excited diary entry, though slightly muddled, gives a clear idea of his strong feelings for Connie, probably having known her for only a matter of months. It is a lovely, excited note to himself (and, maybe, to the biographer he mentioned at the start of his diary). The previous journal entry, dated January 29 1907, made no reference to Connie.

And just as Max is being bowled over by Constance, Constance is letting herself sink into the deliciousness of Kelmscott. She wrote:

*"I shall never forget a studio evening to which I was invited… when for the first time the poems of Rossetti and Morris were read aloud in a beautiful low voice; the studio was shadowy in candlelight and hung with Morris scuffs and furnished with old oak and brass and china. I received an amazing positive sense of beauty that swept over me and drenched me. I beheld a new world hitherto undreamed-of and unvisualised, in which the fairy-tales so dear to children suddenly became alive, lifted completely away from anything I had been able to imagine myself, and revealed, infused with the colour, depth and mystery.*

*…We seem to have stepped into almost feudal peace, and the craftsmanship… delighted us as much as the Tudor manor houses and characteristic architecture."*

This is Constance in a particularly romantic mode, or mood. While she is capable of strong emotions and practical skills which drive her to plan and create a range of projects, we know she is also subject to and has the capacity for whimsical and enveloping mystery: a quality which some of her friends loved and most went along with but others may well have found find fey.

Whichever it was, Connie continued to write. As mentioned earlier, most of her books were written to entertain, and it is fair to say that while many (perhaps most?) readers enjoyed her very individual (and often amusing) work, others did not.

When writer Frank Swinnerton, critic and editor at Chatto and Windus, received a submission he would write a long report weighing up a book's commercial interest against its literary merit. He made it clear that if Chatto and Windus wanted to improve the quality of their publications he said that "these kinds of novels have to go." He turned down at least one of Connie's books.

Max continued to visit galleries, libraries and exhibitions. This satisfied his appetite for culture and helped develop his work. He continued, as usual, to observe and to study diligently. It is right to say that throughout his life he was a polymath, always seeking knowledge about many things other than his painting. The books he wrote reveal his interest in subjects ranging from Fra Angelico to playing the violin to sewing.

Some people would have been surprised at Max's interest in a woman, others would not. The Smedleys would certainly have known or at least known about gay men who were married to heterosexuals. Those who suggest that the combination of Connie's disability and Max's sexual preference for men meant that they could have no children are almost certainly correct, but the subject is unknowable and unknown. Indeed, responding to a request from a gallery for personal details, Max said he did not believe in stating them:

*"as they seem to me no business of the public, but anything in the nature of detail about work or ideas etc. I shall be pleased to furnish you with."*

The important thing was that the pair were enjoying each other greatly, and suddenly marriage was presenting itself as a possible course of action. Connie (now in her early thirties), and others, would have been thinking about marriage long before this. Indeed, when at college Connie must have watched the ease with which some students made and changed boyfriends and girlfriends. How had that made her feel? By now, some years after leaving college, many of them would have had husbands and wives and children.

And what difference did her disability make? Perhaps not much, and as she grew up she must have seen others flourish in circumstances like hers. Those in Connie's parents' position must hope that their child will be cared for when they are gone. Looking ahead, if Connie outlived her parents Di would seem to be a much more likely carer than Billie. As described above, Di was competent in many ways and William Smedley and Annie may well have hoped that Di would find the heart, time and space to make appropriate arrangements for her sister later in life.

Were Annie and William quietly hopeful as they saw Connie and Max's relationship develop? They must have already noticed that a good number of young men found Connie lively and attractive. And now, unexpectedly, a pleasant young artist comes along and wants to marry her. He seems very suitable: he anticipates Connie's every wish, he is well educated, and – crucially important – is very fond of Connie, as she is of him. Also, it soon becomes clear that Max pays constant attention to Connie, anticipating her quite demanding needs.

From the parents' point of view the only thing against Max was that he was, so far at least, unable to earn enough on a regular basis to support himself and their daughter. However, there was no shortage of money in the family. While Connie was a demon at organising other people to get things done, she needed a great deal of help in respect of personal attention because of the damage to the lower part of her body. As her relationship with Max blossomed he undertook an increasing number of tasks, such as getting her in and out of her wheel chair, or a car, or carrying things to and from her, or doing any one of those actions which most people usually carry out for themselves without a thought.

But 1907 and 1908 were not all sweetness and light as can be seen from extracts from Connie's letters.

For example, what is to be made of this unhappy letter that she sent to Geoffrey Whitworth. It was written on April 25th 1908, posted in Florence, and signed Peter, Connie's Kingdom name for herself:

*"Dear Geoffrey,*
*Poor little Max. He has written a postcard to say I show 'ignorant Hate'. Of course he is a crank (?) mystic and I ought to have been patient. But I am going to have trust. I love Max and I want him to be free, and I must face his weakness. I see Hells unveiled here, Geoffrey, and the Hell of sexual perversions is under all this occultism … Oh Geoffrey I love the child Max so much, he has been so unhappy and he will be more so –"*

This emotional letter is confusing and disturbing. Geoffrey was her confidant, but how would he have reacted to these intimate words? The letter is rare in that it mentions the word "sex". It also refers to religion. By this point Max seems to be, at least, a lapsed Quaker, a man interested in the occult, and, to boot, one who Connie knows to be "sexually perverted". And what is meant by Max's "weakness?" Homosexuality? Or something else?

The letter was an emotional over-the top outpouring about the people in her Kingdom, the power and the need for love, her apparent adoration of Geoffrey and her hope that her imaginary world could bring people together. This was all evidence of her unique character. It is hard to decide whether Max really liked this fantastical side of her nature, or indulged her, or hid his irritation. At least he condoned it.

Connie could do nothing about Max while she was in Florence. Would she share all this with her mother? That would have been very surprising, for at this stage she seems closer to Geoffrey than to Annie.

And what does she mean when she says she wants Max "to be free". Free to do what? Or freedom from what? It is true that Connie is some years older than the 27 year old Max, but here she sounds positively maternal.

At this point, while Connie wandered around El Doumo, leaning over the Ponte Vecchio and gazing at the Arno, she must have been pondering another key issue in her life. What should be done about the Lyceum Club, now that it had grown up and become so successful? It meant so much to her. She must have been weighing up the advantages and disadvantages of remaining in her role as Secretary, which was an onerous post. It was Connie's energy and vision that had caused the Lyceum to be born and to thrive, and she and others would have known that her strengths were in inventing and driving projects in their initial stages, rather than in maintaining them. Finally, she was so keen to create more (unspecified) projects unencumbered by the demands of the Lyceum Club that she resigned from her post.

The decision seems to have been a sudden one. It was not unexpected by the club's officers and members, but at least some of those close to her must have recognised that things might well be about to change for her because of Max. Connie did not regret the decision, but first she needed to address the Lyceum's future. Earlier, she had said, "It would be ridiculous to let the club tumble to pieces now". Very luckily for her and the Lyceum, her mother Annie (with help from Di) nobly agreed to take over the Club's significant responsibilities even though she was in her late fifties and lived a busy life.

Connie speaks these words to her mother in the play about Connie written by Frank Hatt:

*"I'm married to the International Lyceum Club. Which is now becoming truly international. Paris, The Hague, Amsterdam. Now Berlin. It's hard work, but it's happening. What appeals, everywhere I go, is the international thing. Reaching out across the boundaries to talk about art and culture and ideas. And it's us women who can do this. Because the men are all so bellicose and belligerent and stuffy and pompous and proud, with their national flags and their armies and navies and all that nonsense."*

*34*

# Weddings

As the letter previously mentioned indicates, Connie and Max must have been getting closer for most of 1907 and at least some of 1908, even if it was an on-off experience. Then, in what feels like a rush, Connie's younger brother Billie married Olive in Paris on the 18th of January 1909. This ceremony was followed a mere two days later by Max and Connie's wedding. The only guests were Geoffrey Whitworth, actor Ernest Benham and Pearl Humphrey, all friends of both Max and Connie. It seems extraordinary that no one from either the Armfield or the Smedley families was present, though Annie Smedley placed this announcement in the Weddings list in the newspaper:

*"ARMFIELD-SMEDLEY On the 20th January Maxwell elder son of J.J. Armfield of Ringwood Hants to Constance, elder daughter of W.T. Smedley of 11 Mecklenburgh Sq. WC."*

There was also an elegant printed card stating:

*"Constance Smedley & Maxwell Armfield send best wishes on the occasion of their marriage, the twentieth day of January 1909. The Uplands, Minchinhampton, Gloster."*

Connie and Max also sent a telegram to Di in Manchester, and a report in a local newspaper carried the following statement.

*"The marriage of Miss Constance Smedley with Mr Maxwell Armfield took place very quietly at a West-end registry office on Wednesday last."*

This was followed by a report which included a brief description of the bride's travelling dress in which she was married, then a small informal reception given by Mrs Smedley at Mecklenburgh Sq. After that the bride and groom motored to Minchinhampton in the Cotswolds.

A paragraph of the report was devoted to Connie's role in having established the Lyceum Club(s) which by then had 3000 members across Europe, and the report writer also commented on her resignation as its secretary as being "a great loss to the club."

This was followed by a paragraph on Connie's role as an advocate of women's suffrage, and mention was made of her earlier successes as a playwright and novelist. But there was nothing at all about Max, the groom. This omission caused at least one commentator to conclude that Connie wrote the report herself, given her penchant for self-publicity.

And why did Mrs Smedley arrange, or agree to arrange, two family weddings so close together? Perhaps it was Connie and Max's choice, but, given that the Smedleys had many friends who might have expected to attend, it is rather strange that it seems there was virtually no sense of celebration.

Then, in January, a deputation of women went to 10 Downing Street. This event led to more public attention, more discussion and more action. The determination of the demonstrators increased, as did that of those who opposed women having the franchise. It was a fraught time, but Constance had not let these events interrupt her wedding and travel plans. Her marriage to Max had taken place at a time when much of the nation's attention was firmly on suffrage action and issues. By now a great deal of publicity had been generated and progress had been made, and it happened that, just a few days before the weddings, the Women's Social and Political Union (WSPU) was actually celebrating the release from prison of two suffragettes.

There is little to suggest that Connie and Max were engaged with the momentous things that were going on in public life. One such event was in 1905 when the Conservative government resigned. It was replaced by the Labour party. Keir Hardie, who had founded the Labour Party, served as its leader from 1906-1908. He was a pacifist as well as a keen supporter of women's rights. What did Max and Connie have to say about that?

While Connie clearly had opinions about demonstrations and arrests and trials and prison sentences, there is little account of her participating closely, except for the brief taste of an event described earlier. Surely these important things were being discussed within her family? And what did the Lyceum Club members make of it all? One would have expected that there would have been tremendous interest and consequent exchanges of a range of opinions, and perhaps there was, but Connie does not appear to be in the forefront: she had already moved on.

When Emmeline Pankhurst was released from prison just one week before Connie's wedding the occasion was celebrated by the WSPU (Womens' Union Social and Political Movement) with energy, hope and determination. At her trial she had announced "*We are here not because we are law-breakers; we are here in our efforts to become law-makers*".

Despite this clear and incontrovertible truth, Connie did not really join in. Was she aware that, on almost the very day when she was getting married, suffragettes were subjected to hideous force-feeding? Certainly, people's private lives had to go on, despite what was happening in public, but Connie seems not to have mentioned the extreme pain that was being inflicted on women by the authorities.

The words "force-feeding", whether read or spoken, bring up horrible images, but these are nothing like as horrible as the thing itself. Connie may not have known what the authorities were doing to keep the hunger-strikers alive, for if any should die while in prison, the government would have been heavily criticised. It was absurd, cruel and shameful.

Force-feeding was illegal – or supposed to be. It consisted of forcing a tube through a nostril, pushing it into the stomach and pouring liquid food down it. If that did not work, the mouth (which the victim would obviously try to keep shut) was prised open so tubes could be inserted and carry food to the stomach. This treatment may have kept some women alive (even though food was often vomited), but it injured many more for years afterwards either because their teeth had been broken, or because food had got into their lungs.

Connie said she wrote daily to the press about women's affairs (a claim which may well be an exaggeration), but two articles she wrote in 1908 were fiery, honest and challenging. At around the time when she appealed to Geoffrey Whitworth because she was confused and worried, she published two serious and substantial articles in a magazine called *Votes for Woman*. One, written in August 1908, has the title *The Matchless Cleansers, Letting in the Light* (this was the name given to a cleaning product of the time). It discusses many aspects of the experiences of suffragettes who were sent to prison, and the subsequent impact on them and on society as a whole. It is a totally coherent and well-thought through sane argument about both the uselessness of force-feeding, and the usefulness of women having the chance to learn at first-hand about prisons. Connie defines prisons as places of hate, whereas they should be places where people are cured. She records how newly released women are feted and welcomed by bands and processions, and how they remain adamant that they will not stop agitating until they get what they want.

In November 1908 Connie wrote another article, this one with the title *To the Impartial Observer*. It asks what all the shrieking and prison business has led to, and states her belief that speeches and actions have actually made a positive difference: men now have a genuine respect for women whose public speaking ability is proven to be equal to that of men. Furthermore, one cannot deny a particularly important fact about the Suffragettes. This is that they have no desire to hurt or injure anyone.

Both of these texts are powerful and persuasive, and it is intriguing to have evidence of Connie's different interests in writing, including her simple child-like stories, novels, thoughtful and contemporary articles, private correspondence and plays. And there is much more to come.

# Country Life and Christian Science

Straight after their wedding Connie and Max settled in the village of Minchinhampton, in lovely Gloucester countryside which Max had previously explored and liked. They lived in a house called Uplands, where they were close collaborators with each other in some projects, and independent artists in others. Max was happiest in the studio at the top of the house where he painted every day, always settled into his preferred steady and almost reverential approach.

While he painted in his studio Connie was at her desk from 8.30 to 12. Together they developed combinations of design, illustration, text and theatre. In particular, they were working on a Flower book, and Connie mentions her pleasure at receiving from her father a book about herbs which was written in 1663.

In 1911 Connie and Max had been married for just two years. The Cotswolds was a very popular place for people in the Arts and Crafts Movement who made – or tried to make – a living from the creative arts, but at this period, although it was a place of beauty and artistic endeavour, it was known equally for its rural poverty and industry. While the mills, in particular, provided steady employment, the income and standard of living of those workers was low.

And the more Connie realised how many local people lived in poverty, the more she moved towards the left. Indeed, she had grown up not knowing about poverty, and though she actually saw the difficulties people faced, she did not at first take much notice of them. It took some time before she chose to look more closely at what disadvantage meant and to do something about it.

Life was going well and Connie's letters to her mother and to her friend Heddie (whose husband Alan Gardiner was a respected scholar) painted a productive yet peaceful household at Uplands. Happily, there was no mention of the difficulties described before her marriage, but of course this did not mean that they had evaporated. Housework was taken care of by a Norwegian maid, and Connie describes a busy life full of good things. She enjoys the house, its situation in the village, going to church, her work, her embroidery, her friends (old and new), a journey on the pony and trap given her by the Lyceum Club as a wedding present and so on. She even uses a tricycle! She sounds both happy and engaged, as one would hope a newly-married woman would feel.

She wrote, *"I've married on practically nothing at all but everything has gone beautifully."*

There is not much about Max (whom she is already enjoying referring to as her husband), other than the good news that he is being invited to exhibit his work, and that it is selling.

The letters from Uplands, written around 1910, carry the first mention of Christian Science. Connie was influenced by two Christian Scientists she and Max met: Heddie Gardiner and, later on in Belgium, a well-known dancer called Ruth St Denis. Until this point Connie attended a local church, but it seems that within a space of only a matter of months the Armfields, rather surprisingly, had adopted new beliefs for themselves, and begun to tell others about their new-found religion.

Christian Science was founded in 1875 in New England by an American, Mary Baker Eddy, who believed that sickness was an illusion that could be corrected by prayer alone, rather than by medical treatment. Ruth St Denis also introduced the Armfields to her vital belief that dance should be spiritual, and should play a part in religion. Both Christian Science and dance became very important to the couple, but Connie was the first to be won over, and it was she who encouraged Max to attend meetings with her.

Connie, though not a regular church goer, would have been familiar with prayers, hymns and sermons while much of Max's knowledge of the Bible had come from studying religious paintings, statues and stained glass windows. Both of them would also have noted that there was less actual *worship* in Christian Science meetings than in conventional Church of England services, that there were no ministers, and that some people (perhaps the majority) attended the church primarily because they were attracted to the fact that peace and wisdom could lead to their suffering – *any* sort of suffering – (whether physical, or emotional) being healed without medical treatment.

However, as time went on, Max had to admit that he was dissatisfied with his work. He attributed this mostly to Connie's acceptance of Christian Science and the consequent pressure she imposed on him. Furthermore, he was advised by Scientists to alter his paintings. Specifically, he was advised to obliterate the "errors" in his work. In this Christian Science context the word "errors" meant shadows, and removing shadows led to Max's work becoming thin and pallid. Years later he jettisoned Christian Science, having recognised that its influence had been negative.

What did Max and Connie make of this "Science" their friends valued so highly? Did Connie consider that her condition could be healed if she (and others) prayed long and hard enough, and lived as closely to the tenets as possible? She had made the best of her body for all of her childhood and youth, but was it possible that God could actually change it? Probably not, but Connie was at a high point of her life: she had a new husband, a pleasant home, enough of what she needed and the opportunity and energy to continue to write. Perhaps it was a time when all things seemed possible. Indeed, in a letter to her friend Heddie she writes "the crutches are burnt – and though I still cling to a stick or a helping hand, the belief in the need of support will surely vanish in the fuller realisation of the light. I do want to hear how you are grounded in Science – I am <u>sure</u> science will wake England! Think how it is a spreading everywhere. We can all carry the light into our corners."

*Letter from Connie to Heddie.*

It seems that there was a Christian Science society in Stroud. Each week there were two kinds of meeting, one with prayers and readings from texts chosen by certain church members, and another predominantly devoted to witness accounts of healing. It seems that Connie attended them both.

# Making the Pageant

Then, in 1911, Connie and Max embarked on the *Pageant of Progress* described in detail through the eyes of a fictitious couple in the Introduction of this book. This extravaganza required a huge and willing effort from both organisers and participants, and gave a great boost of interest and pleasure to them and to its audiences. The following pages give a factual account of how it was made and what people thought of it.

It is not entirely clear who first voiced their suggestion of putting on a pageant. In the Souvenir Programme it is stated that Constance Smedley (Mrs Maxwell Armfield) first conceived the idea. Big pageants were just the sort of thing that Constance would have known about and been interested in, and which she could have worked on with Max. But – and it is a big but – her name does not appear amongst the lists in the official Programme of people who took on the most onerous responsibilities, though it looks as if she played the very minor part in the role of Peace. Just as importantly, the generous amount of attention from the press hardly mentioned her. In contrast Max and the script writer Frank Gwynne Evans were properly recognised and warmly congratulated.

The pageant had needed the collaboration of numerous people. To start with, those in charge made a key appointment: Miss May Cull was to be the Mistress of the Pageant – that is, the director. Also, Charles Apperly (the local dignitary) was to be the Master of the Pageant Ground, Sir Alfred Apperly was to be the Chairman and Treasurer of the Central Committees, Miss Seymour Keay would be Mistress of the Robes and Maxwell Armfield the Artist.

Mr Gwynne Evans was engaged to write the entire script in rhyming verse. Committees were formed to organise publicity, finance and costumes. Local teams took responsibility for the contribution from their particular village. Painswick, for example, organised Episode VI which portrayed Puritans and Royalists in the Election of 1660, and the volunteers from in and around Stroud had to find actors, musicians, painters, designers, stage hands, carpenters and makers of costumes.

It took months of preparation and practice, and, in the event, its three performances in September 1911 exceeded all expectation and proved to be extremely enjoyable, educational and memorable for everyone.

Meanwhile Max, as usual, also wanted to get on with his own paintings. These would have absorbed him totally were it not for the fact that he was the director of all things artistic throughout this pageant. He must have had to abandon his usual work and begun to plan and create colour schemes for costumes, backdrops, set design and more. He was pleased to do so, not least because doing so helped Connie. The evidence is that he threw himself into the project. After all, they had been married for only two years. Whatever he felt, he was successful.

In short, it seems that both Connie and Max were involved with the event in some capacity. It is difficult to imagine that Connie was less involved than Max because their relationship was closely linked to their pleasure and interest in sharing theatrical, literary and artistic activities. Connie's apparently minimal participation may have been because the people appointing those who would create the pageant had much more power, wealth and experience than she did. These personages were, in fact, the local great and the good. Frank Gwynne Evans (admittedly, he was not local) was appointed as the secretary of the Business Committee in addition to his main role as the author of the entire script. Moreover, his wife was secretary of another pageant committee as well as having a role in the drama (years later, Max painted her portrait). Of course the script writing was the very job that Connie might have thought herself able and equipped to do. Indeed she might have coveted that task.

Pageants at that time were very much in fashion. Most of them dealt with the history of a community, involved hundreds of local people in decorative costume, used no professional actors, were held out of doors and gave plenty of entertainment. A few of the many pageants around that time were held at St Albans (1907), York (1909), Winchester (1908) and Southend and Westcliff-on-Sea (1909), and there were more. One man, Louis Napoleon Parker, became famous through writing pageants. So popular was this fashion that the word "pageantitis" was coined to describe "An enthusiastic rise in the popularity of pageants."

The fictional couple at the start of this book served their purpose. They set the scene for *The Pageant of Progress* which turned out to be a highly successful event in the Armfields' lives and an example of what they usually did very well: co-operating on creative projects.

Though it is not known how much Connie was involved in the pageant, she must have influenced it. No one could have failed to notice what was going on and it is extremely unlikely that Connie would have been able to resist joining in. Her aim – in whatever role she claims she had – was not only to create something interesting, enjoyable and memorable, but to create more life-enhancing opportunities and experiences for people whose lives were very limited.

After the final performance in Fromehall Park numerous sincere congratulations were paid to all those who had given so much time and effort. Nine newspapers published reports of the pageant, and these were all enthusiastically positive. As well as recounting the content of the episodes, they commented on the cast lists, the actors' skills and the worthwhile ambition of the whole enterprise.

This rather patronising but supportive extract is from the *Cheltenham Echo*, published after the performance of September 4th:

*"... the pageant will for all time be remembered as a triumph for the working classes of the Mid-Gloucester Division – men who day in and out work in our local mills and factories and women, too, whose life consists in 'plying needle and thread'. How they all worked is a story that will never be forgotten .... Of over 1,100 performers a thousand were drawn from the working classes, and yet how excellently they all did. Optimistic from the beginning they allowed nothing to discourage them."*

And this delightful account is from the *Daily News*:

*"Of the many beautiful tableaux represented, the 'Meeting of Edward III and the Flemish weavers' and 'Queen Elizabeth and the Huguenot refugees' were perhaps the most successful. In the first, shepherds are seen entering with their sheep, and both the men and their quadrupeds filled their parts admirably. Overawed by the approach of the king the shepherds deliberate nervously as to what is the proper thing for them to do to show him they are his subjects 'good and true'. Shall they kneel down or simply take off their hats? Finally they decide upon lying down flat on the grass, although the process seemed even to them as 'summat funny'. The comical way in which they prostrated themselves drew roars of laughter from the audience. As to the sheep they tripped on the stage with the assurance of actors who knew their part perfectly. True they had but little to do, but this they did most conscientiously. The verdant setting of nature in the shape of green grass formed a tempting bait and they broke into little groups and browsed peacefully without any shyness or embarrassment at the storm of applause that greeted this bit of natural acting."*

All in all it is clear that the pageant was a total success for audience, organisers and performers alike. After the many thankyous and the thunderous applause the imaginary couple stood up, and made their slow way across the bare stage along with others. Children peeped into the tents where the actors changed and gave handfuls of grass to the tethered horses whisking their tails. A couple handed in a coronet dropped, perhaps, by a passing earl still in costume. A mother and daughter stood on the stage trying to count the rows of emptying seats. Children insisted on keeping their wooden weapons. All the way home the talk was about the pageant.

# 37

# The Cotswold Players

Once the pageant was over and normal life had resumed there must have been a tangible sense of loss. Given the numbers of people engaged in creating something that they had never seen before and then bringing it to fruition had been a tremendous achievement. The whole event had been built with trust and optimism underpinned by curiosity and urgency. Interestingly, the first question that many potential participants would have asked might well have been: "How can we do this?" rather than "Why are we going to do this?" Somehow, the proposal to do something so unlikely and unexpected had its own energy that leapfrogged over reason and ignored other needs.

On the first occasions when the pageant was proposed, perhaps at some sort of village meetings, people would have had a range of responses. Variously, they might have been astonished, delighted, doubtful and positively anxious.

> *How could our village do that?*
> *What about my job?*
> *What fun it'll be!*
> *It won't work.*
> *Who'll be in charge?*
> *Who'll pay for it?*

And when at last the final performance of a pageant – any pageant in any community – took place, there must have been a lingering heaviness of "It's all over now. What a shame".

But it wasn't over. Pageants left people feeling better. They felt differently about their neighbours and other villages. There was togetherness, and they liked it. Because of the songs and plays, music and poems, they felt differently about their past and their future. Most importantly, they felt differently about themselves. While there may have been some jealousies or upsets en route, the main emotions would have been laughter, fellowship, pride and pleasure in achievement.

So keen were the villagers to hold onto these strong emotions that after the pageant they voiced what they felt to Connie. She was clearly empathetic.

Essentially, they posed a basic question: "Can we do something like that again?" Enough people felt the same, and this led to the formation (it took about two years to achieve) of a group who called themselves The Cotswold Players. It was their positive questions and comments which led Connie to realise that she could make a difference here in the country, close to home.

The group which came together would have been confident about their future because the *Pageant of Progress* had been extremely well reviewed. Many now knew Max and Connie to greet and speak to, and they were nourished by that relationship. Some, at least, of those who had so little must have felt that Connie was "on their side". In the preparations and performances of course there were no "sides" but Connie recognised she that found herself being touched by poverty in a way that she had not been previously. At the same time poor people found themselves in conversation with people they had never spoken to before.

As mentioned before, Connie needed a substantial amount of exposure to poverty before she actually began to understand the lives of others. It was in the Cotswolds when she first realised what poverty actually meant: the millworkers and farm labourers had barely enough to live on, little protection from the weather, harsh employers, and shortages of food, health care, and educational opportunities. And of course, the class system ensured that the rich kept hold of their privileges and advantages while the poor were locked into their fate and their deferential attitudes. Connie could hardly be blamed for being part of that.

# 38

# Post Pageant

In spite of Connie and Max's absences after the pageant, the group of Cotswold Players was eager to put on another performance. They had actors and singers and people keen to make scenery and costumes and yet more volunteers who offered to take care of the publicity. But they lacked something essential: suitable plays.

So Connie found herself writing some short plays specifically to be performed by the newly established Cotswold Players. Worried about how these would be received she first of all rehearsed them back in the Cotswolds in Little Rodborough House (so perhaps visits to Glebe House in London were sporadic?) to which she and Max had recently moved. The players acted them in front of a small and friendly audience, and then they dared to put them on in the local schoolroom, and even charged for tickets. As usual, Max could be relied on to deal with practical issues.

The first programmes presented were *The Ghost* (a Christmas farce set in 1850), *Mother's Rights* (a domestic comedy) and *Pierrot's Welcome* (A fantasy). Connie's encouragement to her actors to use local dialect was popular with actors and audiences.

Clearly, Connie, as usual, was nothing if not versatile and energetic.

The success of the Pageant in 1911 and the plays written after that inspired Connie and Max to develop their dramatic productions into something more substantial, more meaningful and more artistic. The concept was based at least partly on an earlier tradition whereby plays were performed by travelling players. Connie began to compose texts, create characters and direct their movements. Meanwhile Max worked to unite rhythm and colour, verse and staging. And so they drew the various components of drama together and began not only to envisage new dramatic works for the new local group but concepts for a more ambitious project: one that would reach well beyond the Cotswolds.

From time to time, when the Armfields began to miss London they packed up what they needed and decamped for a while. This obviously meant that their contact with Cotswold people was reduced – a situation that Connie, in particular, must have regretted, as did the almost-abandoned Players. Max was more self-contained. Wherever he was he would create a neat, orderly studio and begin to paint. It is certainly the case that he applied his many skills to whatever needed doing: carpentry, cooking, making scenery, arranging music and so on, but what he always wanted most was to paint. This meant that he was often – by choice – alone. He needed his own undisturbed space and time.

The Armfields moved away from the Cotswolds and lived again in Glebe Place in Chelsea. Over the years they moved house several times, often seemingly without explanation, but probably because although the Cotswolds offered peace and domesticity and local friends, London offered energy, artists, more space, bigger audiences, and better opportunities to develop their latest project. In short, it must have felt to the couple that they needed both pastures and pavements if they were to get the most out of life and contribute the most to it. Also, they may well have had financial reasons for chopping and changing between renting or buying.

# 39

# Dance Development

The Armfields were not the only artists involved in theatrical experimentation. Dance was becoming an increasingly important element in London where Margaret Morris, an accomplished dancer and choreographer, was creating alternative programmes, as was Hester Sainsbury. Interestingly, Morris was inventing a system of dance notation: an extremely difficult task which Rudolph Laban (another dancer) was already working on.

In about 1912-14 the Armfields moved yet again, this time firmly back to Glebe Place. In their studio, they decided to develop their work into something more theatrical. Keen to incorporate dance they began to work with Ruth St Denis and her husband Ted Shawn, also a dancer. The pair had established Denishawn, a highly successful and influential dance school and dance company in the US. Max and Connie, influenced by Ruth and Ted, introduced ideas from the far east into their performances. Ruth was particularly well-known not only for her "Orientalism", her feminism and her spirituality, but for her yogic breathing.

These various elements, and others, were being translated into contemporary dance elsewhere. People like Margaret Morris were using novel approaches and methods which were neither classical ballet nor traditional folk dancing, but predominantly abstract movement capable of creating beauty, character, narrative and emotion. Connie and Max, impressed by the new experiments being undertaken in both the UK and the US, began to think more about creating performances incorporating different types of choreography and music, alternative ways of dressing a stage, and of enhancing performances. It was a hugely exciting time for them.

Connie, in particular, experimented with combining art forms, using a variety of tools such as décor, speech, soliloquies, choruses, song, costume and colour. She had wanted to bring art forms together for some time, and now she was doing it. At this time she and Max were not alone in working in little theatres. In London, for example, people were admiring Hester Sainsbury's rhythmic verse poems.

Happily, as war approached, these small, individual arts enterprises managed to keep going. Importantly, most of them were driven as much by the need to express pacifism as by the need for abstract artistic expression.

The Armfields' move did not mean that they turned their backs on the Cotswold Players. When the group needed more plays Connie and Max created more. Some were in a distinctly rural style, and most of them were in rhyme even if that sometimes resulted in a rather unnatural word order. These plays were produced and much enjoyed in Stroud and local villages. Within a few years the Players had secured stages, costumes, scenery, music, props and so on. It must have been quite a time-consuming business, nourished not only by the love of performing and of the theatre, but by friendship and trust – the legacy that Connie and Max were laying down.

Connie had a very hands-on approach, and because her participants were untrained and inexperienced (unlike many of the actors she had worked with) she decided to get them to focus initially on their posture in order to create repose and unity. This, she seemed to believe, would create a starting point for the body. It is not easy to know why she chose posture – rather than, say, gesture or speech, and nor is it clear if she expected doing this to be a straightforward affair, but the process cannot have been so. Undaunted, she embarked on developing a complicated scheme of exercises which could be used either as a tool for classroom coaching, or for individual tuition. Creating this required her to analyse the elements of drama such as: the central idea, method, movement, grouping, colour, music and sound. She listed these and explained how each should be expressed.

# Greenleaf Theatre

The couple decided to set up a new company for their new type of work. It was developed from the more conventional performances practised by the Cotswold Players and they named it Greenleaf Theatre. Their centre was based at The Studio, Mockbeggar Hill, Ringwood, New Hampshire, thus bringing them back into Armfield territory in name if not in body. It seems that they still owned or rented somewhere in Chelsea which was suitable for their rehearsals and productions.

The essence of Greenleaf was to bring all the arts together with the intention of using them to project the central concept of a play. This could be done in a variety of ways. For example, as a character changed their role in a play, their way of speaking and moving would change too, thus focusing attention on the characters and their relationships. In short, the essential questions a Greenleaf director was trying to answer was "What is the idea we are bringing out?" and "Is the idea important?" not forgetting "Is every form of art we use of satisfactory standard?"

But Connie's ambition was not limited to developing the Greenleaf project. She, like others already mentioned, was puzzling over how to record the movements of performers. Words could be learned from the page, but could the body's turns and steps and waves be recorded and then translated into action by someone else? Surely that was not possible?

But Connie thought it was, and she embarked on creating a method for "writing" dance. She and Max must have had long conversations about how best to do this, and the result was Connie's steady symbolic "text" accompanied by Max's stylised images of dancers on the top part of each page of the script; it was these images which told the actors/dancers what they were to do. This often had to be explained and demonstrated by a teacher or repetiteur, rather than working it out from the book alone.

Fittingly, Connie named her detailed and exploratory system *Theatre Elements.* Her series of small books were published by Duckworth. Many actors and those teaching drama must have struggled to understand them. Despite the inclusion of such minutiae, the press reviews about Greenleaf were very complimentary. Connie completed eleven Greenleaf books, and they were found

PUBLICATIONS OF

# THE GREENLEAF STUDIO

MOCKBEGGAR HILL, RINGWOOD, NEW FOREST

TEXTBOOKS

RHYTHMIC SHAPE (A Text Book of Design)     6/-
*Maxwell Armfield*
GREENLEAF THEATRE ELEMENTS     6/- each
*Constance Smedley*

1. Action
2. Speech
3. Production
4. Minstrelsy (in preparation)

GREENLEAF RHYTHMIC PLAYS     1/- each
    1st Series     *Constance Smedley*
1. Belle and Beau
2. The Gilded Wreath
3. The Curious Herbal

    2nd Series     *Maxwell Armfield*
1. The Minstrel
2. The Grassblade
3. Lost Silver

    3rd Series     *Constance Smedley*

1. The Fortunate Shepherds     3/6
    (A Cotswold Pastoral in 2 acts, with 160 illustrations)

NURSERY CLASSICS FOR CHILDREN
*Constance Smedley*
1. Red Riding Hood's Wood     1/-

*All the Above are published by Gerald Duckworth and Co., Ltd., and can be obtained from all booksellers and the Studio.*

*Particulars of Yearly Summer School, August-September, lectures and demonstrations, and lessons and productions through correspondence, from the Secretary.*

*A list of Greenleaf Theatre publications.*

useful by the colleges, universities, theatres, institutes of fine arts, drama leagues and summer schools that Connie and Max worked with when, some years hence, they lived and worked in the USA. They spent time in the following places, and many more besides:

Community Theatre, La Jolla
Evanston Drama League
Chicago Institute of Fine Arts
New Mexico University
Mills College, Mass.

Here is an extract from Connie's book on Production:

*"Let us remember that idea, story, characterisation, atmosphere, have all to be unfolded simultaneously and that the audience must not be distracted from the general purpose of the play by a redundance of detail in any direction. While the audience has its opera glasses on a buhl cabinet*… it is not back in the period: it has been temporarily transported to an antique-shop state of mind. When the house rises with a gasp, like a drawn-out fish, at the silver tissue mantles … do not forget your fish is gasping because it has been drawn out of its natural habitat into an extraneous element. You have hanked it out of the waters of life…"*

This writing is totally different from the first books Connie had written ten years earlier. At best, prose like this is a happy testament to her reputation as an accomplished writer and dramaturge. By surrounding herself with painters, actors, dancers and writers she continued her own personal education in the arts which had begun in her parent's sitting room, was developed at Birmingham School of Art and then nourished by a range of creative people of whom her husband Max was by far the best. Of course there were others who were famous and high achievers, but, in sum, Max was the closest, the most productive and the most significant.

It was not until 1928 that Rudolph Laban succeeded in inventing a notation system for recording and analysing dance. He used symbols, figures, and even letters and numbers to indicate anything from an entrechat to an arabesque. Laban's method, named Schrifttanz (Written Dance) would have had some shortcomings, but it was progress.

---

*   buhl is elaborate and (at the time) fashionable inlaid work of materials such as woods, metals and ivory.

While the Armfields and their friends and fellow-artists were getting to grips with notation, war was looming. We know that Connie did not have strong feelings or much knowledge about politics, though it was the case that she had, over the years, moved to the left. Max could not be described as interested in politics until one reads some of his later, unpublished work. But, as the situation became worse, the couple thought increasingly about leaving England in order avoid the war.

# War Approaches and Move to the U.S.

Unsurprisingly, Max and Connie's fairly detached attitudes towards politics and the declaration of war in 1914 caused them to commit themselves firmly to their decision to go to the USA. One might have thought that Max's Quaker background would have meant he was a pacifist, and he was, but he did not attend a tribunal to register as a Conscientious Objector and perhaps he was not called to do so. The definition of a CO is: an individual who has claimed the right to refuse to perform military service on the grounds of freedom of thought, conscience, or religion. It would be interesting to know precisely how Max defined himself.

Max did not volunteer to work for an organisation such as the civilian Friends Ambulance Unit as some Quakers did. Indeed, there is no evidence that he affiliated himself to the Quakers at all. Moving out of England was possible for him and Connie, though they were aware that it would not be easy. The essential requirement was a passport and passports were very hard to obtain. Previously that had not been the case, but by the beginning of the war it was. As we know, Connie was used to finding ways of achieving what she wanted through personal contacts rather than official channels, and this, it seems, was what happened on this occasion. Passports, against all expectation, were supplied to them as if by magic. There was no visible explanation and no evidence of requests or applications. Clearly strings had been pulled by at least one influential person. The reason for this is unclear, unless it was for a personal favour. But who might have organised it? Was Geoffrey Whitworth, the Armfield's long-term supporter, perhaps the fixer? Obviously, the pair were delighted with their small brown piece of cardboard to which their photographs had been stuck and under which they signed their signatures: Annie C. Smedley and Maxwell A. Armfield. (Annie was, of course, Connie's rarely used given name).

But before they sailed in 1915, with war already underway, they worked on a unique project with Vernon Lee, a poet, traveller and lesbian essayist. She was a key member of a group of artists, writers, dancers and musicians who lived in and around Chelsea and who had all, to some degree, been influenced by the experimental theatre described above. Vernon Lee's most important work was the satirical prose poem entitled *The Ballet of the Nations* and subtitled A *Present-day Morality*. The intention was that it should be a ballet but that was impossible at the time. Instead, the text was published with "a pictorial commentary" by Max. This dealt directly with war and peace presented symbolically. Its characters included Suspicion and Disease, Science and Fear, and its purpose was not the poet's depiction of pacifism and war – though these were both realised in an elegant yet violent milieu – but to prompt readers to reflect on their responses to war, and to prevent the Ballet Master Death from being triumphant yet again. This commission was vital to Max. More than ever, it confirmed and demonstrated his slightly mystical style of painting. His illustrations for *The Ballet of the Nations,* therefore, marked a seminal point in his career. Grace Brockington's book entitled *Above the Battlefield* "explores the crisis of artistic vocation which developed in Britain after the outbreak of war in 1914." It was published by Yale in 2010.

The Armfields travelled to the US on SS *Lapland,* an RMS liner built by Harland and Wolff for the Red Star Line. It was one of the liners that made frequent voyages back and forward across the Atlantic between New York and European ports. Such a crossing must have been quite an adventure, not without some fear attached, for RMS *Titanic* had come to spectacular grief on an iceberg only a few years earlier in 1912. It was *Lapland* that had carried the surviving members of *Titanic's* crew back to England once they had been de-briefed in the US.

By this time the German U boats were beginning to sink ships such as the RMS *Lusitania.* The transatlantic liners were about 300 metres long, and they sailed at about 20/25 knots per hour. The journey to the States was scheduled to take four or five days. Connie and Max were First Class passengers able to enjoy the best accommodation, meals, ballroom dancing (but not for Connie, of course and highly unlikely for Max!), entertainment, observation platforms and more. It is probable that the Smedleys and the Armfields contributed to what must have been hefty fares. They would have wanted Max and Connie to be comfortable and to make the most of the experience.

The couple embarked from Liverpool on April 8th 1916. On the passenger lists Max was listed as "artist" and Connie as "wife". Were any of their parents or siblings there to see them off? Or had they already said their farewells elsewhere?

Either way, the people saying goodbye on the dockside would have been subject to strong emotions, both those who were setting out and those who were being left behind. The crowd on land were waving to families and friends who were setting off across the sea to the new world, and the crowd on deck were waving hats and handkerchiefs. People in both groups were holding up babies, gesticulating, hoping, standing in silence, worrying about luggage and about what would happen, suffering the anticipated loss of people loved. And weeping. And laughing. The size of the ship would have reassured some, while others would be trying to summon up the courage to board.

Connie must have been very excited. She and Max were about to make a new life for themselves in a new country, although they had made no firm plans for staying in the US. While a key reason for their desire to leave England was at least in part, to be safe, they were hungry to embrace the opportunities that such a move offered for their work. It was their first Atlantic crossing and they must have experienced a mixture of anxiety, curiosity and hope. They trusted that they would find contacts who would help them on their arrival, but basically, at the point when they disembarked in New York they would be on their own: ready and eager to bring their talents to the US, and to develop their precious Greenleaf theatre project.

And what did Connie's and Max's parents think? They would have dwelt on the risk, not just of the journey, but of all the future waiting for their adult children. After all, it was the case that Connie and Max might choose to stay there, or that something might go wrong. Each of the four parents must have considered the sombre possibility that they might never see their first-born again.

Of course, Connie and Max might well have thought the same about their parents, but when they sailed past the Statue of Liberty (which Max thought was "*appalling*") towards Ellis Island they would probably have been buoyed up by quickened pulses and a good helping of trepidation. Rumours would have been circulating about which documents passengers should be carrying, about the crowds on the dockside, about buildings they recognised from photos.

*42*

# Letters Home

The present section of this book is based on a pile of about thirty papers – mostly Connie's letters to her mother. They were dirty, torn, and water damaged. Apparently they were found in a skip with other rubbish. As described in the Introduction, they were handed by an unknown woman to Frank Hatt, a writer living in the Cotswolds. The woman had no idea what these papers were (and nor did Frank Hatt), but something about the grubby pile (or something about her, or both) must have caused her to rescue them and give them to someone whom she thought – correctly – might use them or find out where they came from. Some years ago Frank Hatt turned these scraps into a delightful play. The letters do not cover the whole period of WW1, and many are incomplete, almost illegible or undated, but they give at least some idea of what was going on in Connie's and, to a lesser extent, Max's lives when they were in the US.

Fortunately, Connie was an excellent correspondent who wrote regularly to *Dear Mother*. When she wrote to the whole family, she started her letter *Dear people*. Her letters are often long (sometimes six or seven sides of notepaper), and always include something interesting. She recounts in detail many of the great variety of experiences she and Max were enjoying such as being invited to social occasions, noticing the natural world, arranging an exhibition and meeting new people. Her main complaint was about how Americans waste food, but she also commented *"One loses the sense of money over here"* because things cost less than at home. From Manhattan, she wrote to her father to tell him that she had a new publisher.

Connie usually wrote in a very legible and steady hand. Her news was almost entirely upbeat: they are staying in a beautiful place; Max has sold three more paintings, and they are being asked to teach embroidery (and Connie asks her father, please, to send her some books about the history of embroidery), for the pair were now surprised and delighted to be known as "The Armfield Embroiderers". They can see that not only is there a real need in the US for serious decorative work, but that they are able to address that need.

Connie and Max must have prepared a mobile exhibition with examples of various sorts of stitching such as: silk shading, fly stitch, crewel work, needle lace, vermicelli, and goldwork. They would have provided information about types of threads, equipment, tools and patterns. They would also have discussed subjects suitable for embroidery, which traditionally feature something from the natural world, like a leaf. Would-be embroiderers would have heard Connie discuss the cherished aim of "painting with a needle and thread" in order to create an accurate replica of reality. They would also have informed those new to the craft – perhaps warned is a better word – about the time embroidery takes. Someone might, with good reason, be pleased with themselves for completing a small yellow flower in a day and a half, but have failed to realise that it would take many more hours to complete the others in the bunch.

Embroidery, Connie's students would have come to realise, is much more than mere sewing. She herself had learned from William Morris's daughter May that it is a specialised craft, which, when well executed, is quite exquisite and unique.

In 1917/18 The *American Theatre Arts* magazine invited Connie to write an article about Greenleaf. This is what she wrote:

*"With the idea of relating art in some way with the people and reaching them in their houses, schools and public places, we set off to work seven years ago to find what could be achieved with simple materials in a small space, without architectural devices of complex lighting. We began in the ancient town of Minchinhampton, Gloucester, a little stone-built mediaeval place just as it was left by the Flemish weavers 300 years ago, and we discovered that the first element was posture, and that was all that could be got from untrained players. Train them to assume descriptive and expressive posture and have them hold it, and one gets some sort of repose and unity upon the stage."*

But Connie rarely includes any analysis or opinion about her work, or Max's, despite their substantial output in the US, and the fact that they completed *Miriam Sister of Moses*, a notable Biblical drama, several books for children and a few for adults. One might have thought that they – or others – would want to describe their experience of creating these projects. In fact, her letters report how, as time went on, they found themselves being feted and given the warmest of social welcomes at universities, theatres and women's clubs. People wanted to meet the enterprising and accomplished couple they were hearing about on the radio. Whatever the Armfields did drew attention. The Americans, quick to praise, were also particularly impressed by Max's work. Within a few years of arriving and exhibiting he was well enough established to be appointed as a member of the jury and committee of the prestigious American Architectural League, and also the chairman of the Society of the Mural Painters of America.

Committee work requires quite different skills from those needed by artists, and it is interesting to find Max, a focused, obsessive and other-worldly painter, agreeing to participate in activities unlike his usual ones, and ones which he might well have declined had he been in England. But he had been brought up by an excellent example of a committee man: his father. Max had watched his father going to meetings, reading minutes, writing letters and expressing his opinion clearly. He would have been well aware of what committees do and how they do it.

43

# Success

At the end of a year, Max and Connie were congratulating themselves on not only not being in debt, but on having $2400 saved and being in possession of a wardrobe of new clothes. Such a satisfactory situation would have more than pleased them – and their parents – greatly. America was providing them with what they wanted: the opportunity to develop their creative work; interest from readers, audiences, students and teachers and enjoyment of each other. All these combined to build a happy and surprisingly successful outcome. Connie and Max had expected to run the sort of events they had been running in England, and as soon as they were settled and started to do so in the US this raised immediate interest. They must have developed their Greenleaf work, building on what went well and even, at a guess, making things up as they went along. Drama students and others bought tickets, enjoyed the performances, told their friends about this multi-talented couple who provided such novel experiences, and then booked to see whatever it was they had already seen or something else entirely different, and thus their audiences increased.

There were various reasons why the Greenleaf Theatre was so popular. For a start, there was apparently nothing like it in the US. Also, the Armfields' aims were not primarily commercial. Rather, their ambitions were to create, to show something new and to generate discussion about theatre, art and life. It was the achieving of these things which inspired them to go further. So, as well as putting on performances, they – especially Connie – developed a series of immensely popular workshops and courses in various places, ranging from theatres to studios to universities. Connie also wrote what could be described as textbooks, or tutorial books, to be used by lecturers.

And one other factor which may have helped the Armfields was their Englishness, for it is often the case that the accents and expressions used by English people attract favourable attention in America.

In short, the two of them were in their element. Connie wrote home in a letter:

*"We both feel we have a great work before us in bringing better ideals to the world through our particular talents but the way through is by no means easy."*

131

Although she did not define what she meant by "better ideals", one can assume that she was referring at least to fellowship, to beauty and to creativity. She comments here on the difficulty of finding their way through, but, given the fact that she and Max were enjoying greater success than they had in England, it is hard to know what they found difficult.

Max too was at his best: energetic, engaged and earning accurate and nourishing compliments from journalists such as this one:

*"He possesses the eye to see the spiritual content of the most material forms of life in America."*

He sold many paintings. A former director of The Fine Art Society in London considered that his work was so varied that mentioning prices would almost inevitably be misleading. If a work like his 1916 painting *In Central Park* was to come on the market now it would probably fetch in excess of £100,000, but one can still buy his small tempera still lives for single figures of thousands, and drawings and watercolours in hundreds rather than thousands.

Indeed, his exhibition record from his first showing at the Paris Salon in 1904 to his ninetieth birthday exhibition at The Fine Art Society in 1971 is a better guide than a price barometer.

At home in England the Greenleaf Theatre had been a small project, still experimenting and developing. Audiences might have consisted of twenty or thirty people, or even fifty, but in America the productions were put on in bigger theatres and on bigger stages with bigger audiences.

Their theatrical work had one particularly prestigious high point. Connie and Max were invited to put on a play, *Miriam, Sister of Moses,* in the Greek Theatre in the University of Berkeley, California. This is a huge open air amphitheatre which seats almost 6000 people. What an experience! What an honour for Connie and Max! Performances, involving a dozen or so characters and about fifty dancers were held, according to the programme, at Eight-Thirty o'clock on August 1st and 2nd 1919, with Ruth St. Denis and Ted Shawn in the main roles.

Connie wrote to her family in green ink:

*"Dear People, An extraordinary success! I wish you could have seen those thousands listen for those 5 acts in that huge amphitheatre!"*

She ends *"we are very very very happy and well."*

*44*

# Omissions

However much Connie's parents must have been delighted by Connie's enthusiasm, they must also have wished that she would have included some detail about these particularly memorable occasions. Yes, her letters left things out but it must also be remembered that the "collection" of correspondence cannot have been comprehensive because that found pile of almost-destroyed papers was a random selection, preserved by a string of lucky coincidences. Who knows what other letters were written by Connie, and lost? Nevertheless, it is interesting to note what Connie seems to have omitted. To start with, while she shares so much information about what is going on in the part of the US she happens to be in, she shows virtually no interest about the activity in the Smedley household or in England – let alone in other parts of Europe. Admittedly, there is some reference to the power of Christian Science, and the pain William Smedley seems to have experienced for a long time (Connie urged him to "Just try it!"). But one can see that she and Max focused almost entirely on their own activities in the US.

It is noticeable that Connie makes little reference to the war, other than a mention of rationing, and of her nephew Hugh (Di's son) who was an army medic in France responsible for examining thousands of troops for renal disease. Connie called the war "a nightmare" but there is hardly a word about fighting and death and slaughter or the progress of the war except, perhaps, her labelling of Germans as "wretched misguided people who are going to get their full punishment". Atypically she adds "I suppose one hates and feels vindictive as long as one secretly fears and feels helpless."

Are these attitudes compatible with her interest in Christian Science? They are certainly very different to Max's former Quaker beliefs. Has Connie, in the excitement of the art-world success that she and Max are enjoying, virtually *forgotten* the hideous war in Europe, or has she dismissed it deliberately because it is a long, long way away, and she can do nothing about it?

Did she not read nor hear conversations about some of the most famous battles such as the Somme and Verdun? About many thousands of military and civilian victims? And what about the important event in 1917 when the US entered the war? She seems not to have mentioned these things.

133

And did she celebrate and rejoice when (most but not all) English women gained the right to vote in 1918? And when American women achieved suffrage in 1920? Some fifteen years earlier she had been involved with the Women's Movement, yet now in the US those issues hardly seem to matter to her. But of course it must be remembered that one has no idea how much correspondence was lost or destroyed.

# More About the U.S.

In the US she found herself very much in her own familiar middle-class social setting, albeit the American version. Some of her attitudes to the big public concerns of the time were unsophisticated and based on simplistic opinions, such as when, in a letter home, she says "I admire England for its inability to bear malice and its genius for shaking hands and making friends once right has been established." What was she talking about?

One gets little sense that she is interested in or in touch with what was happening in the world other than through newspaper headlines, but perhaps she may have deliberately decided to write optimistic letters rather than unhappy ones. Who can blame her for wanting to enjoy her peaceful life in the US? After all, the main reason why she and Max came was to avoid war.

This visit to the States sounds altogether action-packed and positive. The couple could measure success by the number of paintings sold, the size of audiences and the attendance at lectures and courses. If things went wrong, they must have found ways – and helpful Americans – to put them right. Connie did not let up. She thought that each US city they visited needed "a new attack", which was her way of describing how she must write and Max must paint in order to make a bold impression when arriving in a new place.

Interestingly, in one of her letters Connie refers to previous difficulties and disappointments which, she claims, she and Max are only now overcoming. Of course when they were still in England they would have liked their work to be better known, but they had certainly not done badly.

All in all they were surrounded by hospitable well-wishers and generally fêted. These years must have been the most exciting ones of their lives. Certainly, it was all a huge contrast to life in the Cotswolds. While it was true that both of them would have been proud to see people admiring their work, they were not used to fame – the word "fame" is used here both cautiously and accurately – but it is not too strong a word for this American adventure.

In another letter she states that in the US there is absolutely no business or financial panic or fear of any kind "except that Max has taken out his first naturalisation papers." One cannot be sure what this sentence implies but it is interesting because Max would surely not do that unless he was contemplating staying in the US. However, a few years after the war ended it was he who was the keenest to return to the UK, while Connie was reluctant. The truth may be that because they had the option of remaining or leaving, they would at times have favoured one course of action, and at other times another. The safest thing was therefore to keep their options open.

# Santa Fe

One of the most special features of Max and Connie's visit to the US was their decision to take up the Santa Fe Railway Company's generous offer to give them a free trip across the States in exchange for art work done en route. The Company's intention was to display the art back in the east so as to encourage visitors to explore the west by train.

Once a spur line had been added to the railway which already reached the Grand Canyon, the Company began to send artists on three-to-four week excursions (to include ten days in the Canyon itself) to record the scenes of its beauty and majesty in paintings, photographs and lithographs. These were to be displayed in museums, in books and in eating places, and, as predicted, they made a real impact on those who saw them.

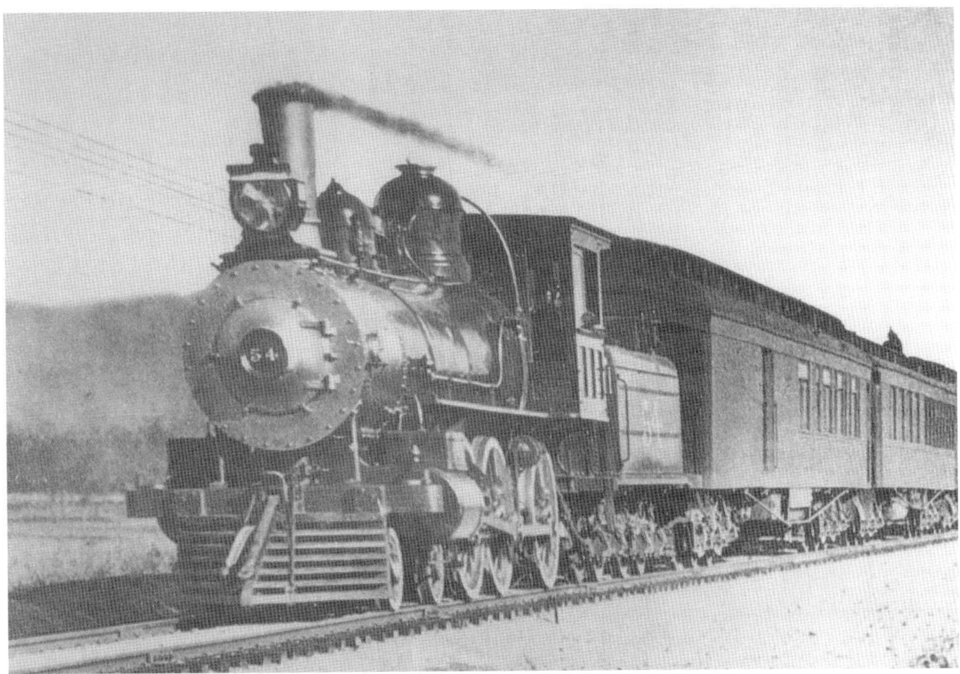

*Santa Fe train.*

Connie and Max were quick to grasp the opportunity inherent in such an offer. But the deal was even better than they expected. For a start, they had a private Pullman carriage – a sort of lounge-cum-studio where they could set up their easels and work. Over and above that, meals were served (sometimes very elaborately at beautifully kept station platforms, sometimes in the train) as was the excellent hotel accommodation. The El Tovar was famous for its comfort and elegance and renowned for its unique site on the rim of the Grand Canyon. Built in 1905 it was described as being in complete harmony with its surroundings – on one side is the great gorge, on the other, a forest. The whole place must have presented an almost unimaginable and astounding display of natural beauty. Max and Connie would have been almost overwhelmed. The sky, the rocks and the earth, all combined with colour, shade and sunlight, formed an exceptional sight. People were interested to see what a British artist made of the US, as this newspaper article evidences:

*"When he comes to California he is fascinated by the strange new vegetation, the ragged eucalyptus, the flaming bark of the madrone trees. Or the weird effect of drifting sea-fog over burnt-up hill, or a volcanic sunset or scarlette butte rising from the pearly desert, making decorative patterns. Again the American Indian attracts him. In one picture he shows a group of women returning with their burdens along a narrow path in the Grand Canyon, Arizona while snowstorms whirl about the distant rocks and the sides of the canyon crowd in with overpowering somberness."*

One particularly successful result achieved under this Santa Fe scheme was the creation of calendars illustrated with paintings painted – or at least begun – by artists when on the journey. Many artists focused on portraits of the local population, or scenes, or abstract patterns based on craft items such as rugs, clothes, utensils. The experience caused Connie and Max to reflect on the visual, cultural and material differences between this part of the US and England. Indeed, life itself was completely different.

On and off the train, Max and Connie must have enjoyed the company of at least some of the other artist-travellers, though Max's priority would have been to paint rather than socialise.

It has been impossible to find out which train or which route or date the couple travelled on, but the train carried them through the territory of various tribes such as the Hopi, the Navajo and the Apache. The painters were keen to paint the faces they saw – so different from those they were used to – and before long the artists found that local people were expecting to be paid for modeling, even when there was just a hint of them being asked to sit for a painting or photograph.

In his book *An Artist on America*, (published in 1924) Max devotes a whole chapter to "Indians" (sic). He states that American aborigines are not Indians, and even to use the word *Amerind* is equally incorrect. However, he uses it elsewhere. The people he meets are of diverse cultures, with different languages and different arts. He describes them clearly as strange and exotic, and admires them as accomplished artists. He and other painters made striking portraits and figures of these people they also called, variously, natives, Mexicans, American Indians and Hispanics.

It is interesting that, in addition to these peoples, he must also have come across many black people in New York and other cities, and they do not feature in his paintings.

Why not?

By far the majority of the portraits and figures he painted were friends, relations and characters from life, legends, history and his imagination, and they were almost all white. Was Max's decision not to paint black people because he considered them visually uninteresting? Or did he consider them of less value than white people? He was brought up to value equality, and to understand that "there is that of God in every man". But of course he was as likely to have contradictory beliefs and actions as anyone else. It is difficult to know, and it would be interesting to know what Max would have said if he had been asked why, when in New York, he had not painted anyone who had black skin – except for a woman in the foreground of Central Park, one of his most famous paintings.

All in all the Santa Fe trip must have been memorable as education, as personal enrichment, as artistic inspiration and as a huge adventure. What an experience.

# Return to England

The relevant ship's list states that Connie and Max sailed back from New York to Southampton on the eleventh day of the eleventh month, in 1921. Remembrance Day had only been firmly established two years earlier, and the couple could hardly have realised what changes the war years had meant, especially as they were travelling on the luxurious RMS *Olympic*. This cruise liner *(Titanic's* sistership, nicknamed *The Old Reliable)* was the largest and best appointed cruise liner ever built. The pair must have been delighted and intrigued by its marble features, its gold embellishments and its plush furnishings. As it approached Southampton it is likely that Connie and Max would have been thinking about their families rather than those who had lost their lives in the war.

Max's family was almost bound to have been at the port to meet the ship, for Ringwood is only about 50 kms from Southampton. They must all have rejoiced to see each other again for it had been a long time apart. The older couple must have noted slight changes in Max and Connie's relationship with each other, in their appearance and in their plans for the future. In the same way Connie and Max might have seen their parents, after the seven year gap, in a different light.

There are two accounts about where Connie and Max went to live on their return in 1922, and their subsequent moves. The most definite is that they moved into the building site which would become Mockbeggar, a beautiful, classic, redbrick house in the Cotswolds. Apparently they built it with help from Harold, Max's younger brother.

It had a lovely garden where the children put on plays. Seven-year old Diana recalls playing the role of Peaseblossom in Midsummer Nights Dream, excited to show off her costume. But Max and Connie did not settle in Mockbeggar because it was too isolated. It seems as if their house at Uplands (an earlier one they liked a lot) was also unavailable, so perhaps they had rented it rather than owned it. In any event the pair seemed to go house hunting often, and in the 1930s they found somewhere to rent in West Wycombe in Buckinghamshire. It was a former pub which seemed to be known by two names – *The Black Boy* and *Old Coaching Inn*. Its most recent occupant was a District Nurse, and it was owned by the National Trust (as was some nearby land) and available at £10 per week.

Connie probably had plans for Greenleaf and more when she returned full of energy and stories from America, but she and Max may have needed to catch their breath while they acclimatised themselves to post-war Britain. At first, it must have seemed as if it was not going to be easy for them to be as they used to be, and do as they used to do. Or, at least, do as they did in America. This may have been linked with finance, with changes in the way dramatic performances were staged and books published, and perhaps with Connie's gradually failing health.

But well before they moved there, the Armfields' obvious priority was to pick up the threads of their previous work. They must have come back full of stories about their successes and hungry to create more, while recognising that their success in the US could not be replicated in England. But Max, first and foremost a creative person, immediately resumed his artistic endeavours. As earlier, some of his work was done in cooperation with Connie, some on his own.

Max's ability to pick up his painting again is evidence of his single-minded focus, his wealth of ideas and his resilience. Clearly, the mystical side of his reverence for his art – both significant qualities – underpinned all of his work.

Bernard Dunstan (Diana Armfield's husband) admired him greatly. He wrote:

*"The strong sense of design and colour harmony in his paintings was always closely related to the philosophical beliefs and principles which he worked out in his many writings. His life was very much all of a piece in this respect on painting, music, poetry, indeed his whole way of being, formed a single whole in which every part was harmonious and interdependent."*

Why the Armfields wanted to be in Wycombe is unclear, as they seem to have had no particular connection with the place, unless Max already knew about the local underground passages and large caverns known as the Hell Fire Caves. These were manmade in about 1750, and are said by some to be haunted – a fact which may well have attracted Max, for on the couple's return from America Max's interest in the occult grew to become a very significant feature of his life.

But perhaps they just went there because they liked the house and could afford it. Whatever the reason, they decided to rent it, and resolved to buy it when they could. This meant that Connie had to ask Di, Di's husband and their son to stand as referees. This was agreed to and it was arranged that Max and Connie should have a trial month in the house. They obviously liked it, for they stayed on and their stay there was probably one of their most settled times.

However, correspondence in the late 1930s and 40s revealed more addresses. Some of these houses were very close to each other, and some were in the area they used to live in:

2 Garden Court, Clarendon Road
14 Crescent Mansions, Elgin Crescent
3 Key House, Chelsea,
39 Glebe Place, Chelsea
Ebblake House, Verwood, Wimbourne.

48

# Grace Darling

Connie's other penultimate book was *Grace Darling and her Islands.* Published in 1932, it was about a real girl, who, with her lighthouse-keeper father, saved a group of sailors from a deadly storm in the Farne Islands in 1838. Huge publicity meant that she became known as a sea heroine. Connie held Grace in great esteem, so much so that she founded the Grace Darling League and became its Honourable Director, while Max was the Chair of its Executive Committee. It is not possible to know how much work this involved, but the rules stipulated that the League should exist for a period of five years: 8th September 1933 to 8th September 1938. Its three objectives were:

- *to establish Grace Darling in history as our sea heroine*
- *to build a Memorial Museum at Grace Darling's birth place*
- *to promote our shipping and navigable waters*

One of the other actions Connie proposed was to have an oak tree planted in every English port in memory of Grace. This was agreed to, and the first tree-planting ceremony was in 1934, in Battersea Park. Participation by women was encouraged by the authorities and was evident by the large number of women who attended, including those from a rowing club (who carried their oars over their shoulders), Dagenham Girl Pipers and Sea Rangers.

A further late initiative was in 1938 when Connie and Max founded a Play Centre in London. This was not somewhere for children to play – though, to a contemporary reader, the words "Play Centre" suggest that that might be the case – but a place where plays promoting thought and inspiring action in the community might be read aloud and studied. Not surprisingly, the first reading was of Connie's own play *Eight Heros and a Heroine,* which told the story of Grace Darling's heroic rescue described above.

49

# Crusaders

Connie did not throw herself back into writing as intently as she had done twenty or so years earlier. Of course she was older now, and she was not well. One of the reasons for this may have been that her mother died in 1923. It is hard to know how close the mother and daughter were, but the death may well have affected Connie.

At this stage of her life, other than children's books, she produced just two notable titles. The important one was *Crusaders*, which held Connie's detailed reminiscences. It was published in 1929.

The book is written in a straightforward style, but because it rarely includes dates, it is, rather frustratingly, often difficult to know the order of events. It is packed with anecdote, opinion and self-reference. But more of a worry for those who read it is the question of Connie's veracity. She seems to embroider events or state that she was more involved in some episode than she actually was, thus making herself appear more important and have a bigger role than was the case in whatever had been going on. The biggest example of this is the contrast of her own account of the *Pageant of Progress* with that published by others. In short, the fact that she presents herself as an unreliable witness and reporter raises doubts about the whole book.

In it Connie described her involvement with the pageant, stating her closeness to its creation and preparation. Indeed, she states, *"The organising was my affair"*, and that she *"planned episodes with Frank Gwynne Evans"*. These announcements, oddly, contradict the evidence in the Programme, but they are not so odd when one discovers that she was judged by some (notably her niece, Barbara MacLean, and Dr. Grace Brockington, an academic and authority on Connie Smedley), to be an accomplished self-publicist, and that not everything she wrote was entirely truthful. But another reason for the absence of evidence of what she did, or might have done, was perhaps due to the fact that she was a woman, and as long as pageants were considered to be the territory of men, women could be rendered invisible. However, there were plenty of women whose participation was championed in this pageant, including the popular May Cull, the Pageant Mistress and Seymour Keay, the Mistress of the Wardrobe.

Another feature of *Crusaders* is that she describes some things in detail while giving minimal – or no – attention to others. For example, the years that Connie and Max spent in the US were really significant, but she devotes only a few pages to them. It is odd that those fruitful and enjoyable years were given so little attention, especially as they were so remarkably successful. These pages come close to the end of the book, almost as if the topics they covered were an afterthought. In fact, *Crusaders* was published about seven years or so after her return from her visit to the US with Max. One would have expected that some of the highlights of such a vital experience would have remained in Connie's memory and constitute a *pièce de résistance* in her reminiscences.

But once one understands a little about Connie's style and character, one can read parts of *Crusaders* with a pinch of salt. Interestingly, that tendency to be economical with the truth does not detract from the book. Rather, it tells us more about Connie: it is quite clear that she wants to be well-thought of; she is warm to the many people she comes across; and she certainly makes the most of her life.

Nevertheless, there are surprising omissions. She says very little about her family, and hardly mentions the substantial periods of illness she experienced during her life. And why should she do either? They seem important to the reader, but perhaps they were not to Connie. Strangest of all, her devoted husband Maxwell Armfield is almost entirely absent. Given his decades of caring for her, his ministering to what must have been innumerable requests, his total cooperation in their projects and their sound friendship, it is sad to reflect that Connie hardly mentioned him. She liked to write about herself, and, to a certain extent, about others, but not about Max. Max must have been well-aware of this throughout his marriage, but it appears that he did not let it upset him.

# Events in England

When the couple arrived back from the US in 1922, the first Hunger Marches were underway. Thousands of unemployed, working-class people were demonstrating about their condition. One of the most dramatic and public methods of drawing attention to themselves and their cause was to march to London. There was little disorder, and they were treated with empathy and even respect.

The Jarrow March took place some five years later when two hundred participants carried a petition to the government, asking for industry to be re-established in Jarrow. They marched from Tyneside to London. The cloth-capped, highly motivated marchers made headlines as they walked in organised ranks with banners saying "Jarrow Crusade". At times they sang, and at times they were silent except for the sound of their footsteps. Like Connie, they considered themselves to be crusaders, albeit very different ones with very different aims and methods to the ones she had in mind. They succeeded in delivering their petition, but it was never debated. It appears that neither Connie nor Max paid much attention to the March or its purpose.

Indeed, they found themselves happily involved with another organisation: the BBC. In the period between 1924 and 1930 they – particularly Max – gave short talks and play readings. Max contributed to several episodes of a programme called *Scholars' Half Hour*. The titles of his talks included *Art in Education*, *Art in Town*, and *Why Bother about Art?* He also composed music for some of these productions.

Meanwhile Connie resurrected the Greenleaf Players and directed programmes of *Belle and Beau*, *The Two Gentlemen of Verona* and various plays for children. She also gave a talk about embroidery.

An example of this partnership with the BBC was on May 26th 1927 when there was a Radio Broadcast from BBC Cardiff, advertised thus in the *Radio Times*, which was then known as *The Official Organ of the BBC* (and was first published in 1923):

*"The Synopsis was a mixed programme composed of music, talk and performance. The Station Trio plays 'Music of Elizabethan Days', the Greenleaf Players perform*

*scenes from Shakespeare's Two Gentlemen in Verona (I ii, II vii, IV iv) and Constance Smedley discusses 'The Women of the Play' and 'Ideals of the Play'."*

The two actors were Betty and Joan Rayner, sisters born in New Zealand. Joan, who could hardly have known Connie although she was Connie's goddaughter, went to London where she worked with Connie, and then returned to New Zealand and founded a Theatre for Youth in Australia. The sisters made a living based on performing plays to local audiences. They were also Christian Scientists.

Max continued to paint, and in 1927 he painted *Miss Chaseley on the Undercliff* (the Undercliff is a particular and popular part of the coast at Bournemouth). Essentially, the portrait is of an older lady, a widow. She used to be Max's housekeeper, and he thought highly of her. Dressed in black she is centre stage, sitting calmly and reflectively while younger people are just behind her and there is a boy playing with a toy boat in a pond. The background is of very green attractive plants, trees and hills.

It was done in tempera, and in 1937 he wrote this account of his use of colour:

*"The flesh throughout was done over a modelled under-painting of black and white, in the Flemish manner. The emulsion used was a mixture of egg yolk, spike oil and Block X amber in linseed. The bright greens were painted with Cobalt Green and in some cases Terra Verte with an overpainting of Alizarin Green and Aureolin in places. The yellows were Pale Y Ochre: Raw Perigod and Roman O. The flesh mostly Raw P. And Pale Ylol and purple Madder."*

# Slowing Down

After the Armfields had been back in England for some years, Connie's rate of creative writing began to slow down. Was that to do with the content she was thinking about and wanted to put on paper, or to the practical difficulties of getting comfortable and having things within reach, or her worsening eyesight? Whatever it was, things were not as straightforward as they used to be.

A significant action Max took at this point was that he – but not Connie – abandoned Christian Science. This led to "an amazing flow of inspiration".

The Armfields' social life, at least at first, must have diminished because they were in a completely new place where it appears that they knew no-one. Wycombe is miles away from Minchinhampton, and Connie was becoming less and less mobile.

This was happening at a time when the Depression of the thirties which followed the Stock Market crash of 1929 must have impacted on the Armfields' life, for, even if they had returned solvent from the US, this might not have remained the case for long. But did Connie have royalties coming in? Perhaps Max was exhibiting and selling his work? Or, had they saved money from their time in America? Whatever the situation, it seems that they were often short of money. Nevertheless, they got by with some funds from Di.

Every now and again the Armfields would employ a maid. Money must have been a factor in deciding whether or not to have one, but so was Connie's sometimes tricky management. She was an unconventional employer whose servants were sometimes subject to unorthodox situations. These were not always resolved to the satisfaction of both parties, so problems were not infrequent.

In respect of the fortunes of the Lyceum, Connie was of course no longer part of the organisation she had once put so much into. On hearing that the club went into voluntary liquidation in September 1934, she must have had at least two responses. Firstly, a justified surge of pride at having created the club; secondly a sigh of regret and perhaps also a sigh of relief that there was no more to be done. The club had lasted for exactly thirty years and, unknown to her (and many others) would be revived in a different format at a later date.

Max's parents' home was within reach of quite a few galleries and exhibition spaces not far from Bournemouth, and on those occasions when Max was at Ringwood he made contact with them. In particular he became a professional friend of Norman Silvester, the curator of art at the Russell-Cotes Art Gallery from 1932-1958. Norman Silvester was keen to encourage local and contemporary artwork by supporting the Bournemouth Arts Club. Hopefully, he would have provided Max with some companionship.

One feature noticeable at around this time, when Max was submitting or loaning more paintings to exhibitions, or selling them privately, was the amount of administration that he had to do. For a start there was quite a bit of correspondence. Then paintings had to be packaged, transit arranged, dates organised, catalogues and forewords written, leaflets distributed, the press contacted, articles printed, prices negotiated, insurance and copyright arranged, payments made. On one occasion the glass on a painting broke when it was in transit, requiring time and energy to sort it out. (This painting happened to be a portrait of Mrs Gwynne Evans, painted by Max decades earlier at around the time of the *Pageant of Progress*. It was her husband, Frank Gwynne Evans who had written the entire script of the pageant).

Did Max wish he had someone to help with this? Perhaps not, for he was very self-sufficient. Connie did what she could to help. For example, she was keen that paintings should be given to other countries as a gesture to promote good international relationships, so she established contacts as she had often done before.

King George V died at Sandringham in 1936, after a brief illness. There was some suggestion that his death was hastened by his doctor. At that time euthanasia was hardly known about, and most people would have considered it a crime. What would Max and Connie have thought about it? Did it make them think again about Christian Science, and about how they had embraced it and then rejected it?

And what might they have thought about Amy Johnson, the aviator, who made longer and longer distance flights during the 30s but who disappeared from the sky above the Thames Estuary in 1941?

52

# Connie's Last Days

Once Max and Connie had settled into the Old Coaching Inn in West Wycombe, they managed to establish a home in which they could make some attempt to continue their arts activities. They wanted to get stuck into interesting and creative work but Connie was no longer young, and her health was still poor.

So it seems that life in the Old Coach House became rather inward-looking and had limited contact with the outside world. As time went on Connie's health deteriorated further, and it seems as if things became really serious at the end of 1940, when Max occasionally called in a nurse to visit Connie. Did a Christian Science practitioner visit her? Quite possibly, because it seems that Connie, whom Di described as obviously very ill, refused to receive medical treatment. Di's husband, Hugh, a highly experienced medical researcher, was appalled by the "care" that Max had provided and said Connie should be in a nursing home. He knew at once that Connie's bedsores were "terribly septic". Connie then had two heart attacks in quick succession, and she died on March 9th 1941.

Notes in Di's diary record her mixed feelings: first and foremost she was angry about the regrettable condition Connie was in. Simultaneously, she also recognised that Max had done what he could: he had done his best.

Sadly, reflecting on Connie's death, Di also acknowledged that she and Connie had not been close.

Ken, one of Di and Hugh's children, supported his mother when he saw her in distress. Sensibly, he reminded her of how Connie used to cause problems at times – problems which required at least time and attention – and pointed out that she would no longer be suffering. He also remarked that things would have become much harder if Max had died before Connie.

Arrangements were made for the funeral to take place a few days later at St Lawrence's Church at West Wycombe. Those present were Max, Di and Hugh, Pearl Humphrey and Geoffrey Whitworth. The last two had attended Max and Connie's wedding in 1909. Also present was one of Connie's nephews, and a grandnephew.

On a tower on the top of West Wycombe church there is, astonishingly, an elegant hollow wooden ball covered in gold leaf, measuring eight feet in diameter.

It is supported by a wooden frame and it was built in the 1700s for Sir Francis Dashwood who owned the church. He wanted a golden globe to rival the bell tower in Venice, upon which stands the archangel Gabriel. Connie, Max and those who lived locally may have taken it for granted, but first-time visitors to West Wycombe tend to find it a very special beacon of beauty. It seems fitting that Connie was buried in the graveyard of a church displaying such an adornment, which, like her, was unique, eager to be noticed and capable of generating delight.

After a good number of years, when the grave had become overgrown and in need of repair, the International Lyceum Club paid for it to be renovated. A group of members from various countries attended an outdoor ceremony and then a service in the church.

53

# David's Ending

But what of my father?

How was his life progressing?

One evening in March, after putting the children to bed my mother settled down to write a letter to Walter D. David and Walter had continued their correspondence for several years since the end of the war.

*Walton-on-Thames*
*March 26th 1949*

She wrote:


*Dear Walter,*

*I hardly know how to tell you my news. Some weeks ago David became ill and went into hospital where he received the best medical attention and every kindness, but he rapidly became worse – with cancer of the liver – and on March 15th he died very peacefully.*

*He did not know the nature of his illness and made a most valiant struggle for his life. He knew though, that he might not recover, but he was full of faith and confidence in God's love whatever should happen. His courage and wonderful spirit were an inspiration to everyone. I spent the last five days at the hospital to be with him.*

*I cannot tell you of my grief or the sadness I feel that you and he who remained close friends through such difficult times will never meet – we must believe, as my darling David did, that everything that happens comes within God's loving care though we may never be able to understand.*

*With sincere good wishes to you all,*

*Phyllis*

My father died when he was 45 years old. His body was cremated and his ashes were scattered in the garden at Esher Meeting House. His immediate family was small; it consisted of my mother Phyllis, my two brothers Gordon and Roger, and myself. There were no grandparents nor aunts nor cousins. Our only uncle, Eric, who had been in the Sheffield City Battalion, had been killed on the first day of the Battle of the Somme. And James had died years earlier.

Fortunately the Quakers gave my mother some funds, making it possible for all three of us to go to Sidcot, as my father hoped we would. This meant that – although of course I could not have known it unless and until I had researched this book – we sat in the same classrooms, ate in the same dining hall and went to art classes in the same art room as Max had done. Of course I was doing those things 50 or 60 years later than Max but this connection pleases me, and I like to think that Max – as well as my father – would also be pleased if he knew that his friend's children went to the same school as he did. He would certainly be interested.

David had left very little money, so my mother had to find a way to make some. She decided to take in lodgers (though we called them "paying guests" because that sounded better) and on the whole it worked well. Over the years, different PGs came for various lengths of time. Several of them remained in contact with us for years. Of greatest importance was the fact that the income they provided enabled us to continue to live in our pleasant house which suited all of us well and which was our home until Gordon, Roger and I were all adults.

*54*

# David's Letter to His Godson

*Written on March 15th 1942*

Our family had lived close to some particularly good friends for a number of years. The Piercys had three children of almost exactly the same age as my brothers and I. Happily, their parents supported us and our mother before and after David's death. Neil, the third child, was my father's godson, and in 1942, when he was 37, David determined to mark Neil's 16th (future) birthday in some way, as he approached adulthood.

He decided to write a special letter, and this is the first paragraph of the first page of the ten page handwritten letter he wrote.

On the envelope it said:

*Neil Douglas Scott Piercy*
*Not to be opened until 15th May 1958*

*Neil,*

*This is a sort of fourth dimensional letter. Most letters are from a person in one place to a person in another place. This is from me in 1942 to you in 1958. From me aged 37 to you aged 16. If I waited to write until your 16th birthday I'd be 53. Perhaps as 37 is much nearer to 16, I may in some ways be able to write you a better letter now than when I'm 53. Beside, the world is an uncertain place these days, and further I am a "poor risk" in insurance jargon: I may not get as far as 53, so it seems a good idea to discharge any godfatherly duties now while the going's good!*

It is a marvellous letter. In it my father writes about subjects as wide-ranging as what was happening in Stalingrad, smokeless fuel, Waterloo Bridge, race relations, barrage balloons and more. He also describes a typical day travelling into London by train from Walton-on-Thames and then walking across Hungerford Bridge to his office, and, at the end of the day, returning home and helping to put the children to bed.

He also asks Neil questions: *"Now, how goes life in 1958? Is it a brave world?"* *"Is it a new world?"* *"Are new forms of beauty crystallising in your tomorrow out of the melting pot which is ours today?"*

My father also enclosed a copy of Lewis Mumford's *The Culture of Cities* and, keen for his godson to understand what was in the news on his 16th birthday, he also put into Neil's parents' safekeeping not only this special letter, but copies of six up-to-date publications (for example *The Times, The News Chronicle, Picture Post*) that would help him, when a young man, to know some of what had been going on abroad as well as at home.

David urged his godson to:

*"Take life, O sixteen year old Neil, with that young mind and spirit of yours and with those two young hands, and find its abundance. Abundance of work to good ends, abundance of happiness in your work and play, and in your home. There you've made a happy landing to start! And if sorrow and tribulation come your way, then be abundantly strong and of good courage."*

He also reminds Neil that *"the artist is not a special kind of man, but every man is a special kind of artist"* words written by Ananda Coomaraswamy, an Indian philosopher and historian admired by Max as well as David.

As Max and Connie did not have children, we can only guess what they would have been like as parents, but I find the mood and essence of David's advice to Neil to be sound, loving and supportive. He was, in his gentle way, doing just what a godfather is supposed to do: urge their godchild to live and to thrive.

At the end of the letter David writes that he would like to give Neil *"a light word"* about one other source of wisdom. He means the quote from Philippians 4.8 which begins with the words: *"Whatsoever things are true"* and ends: *"Think on these things"*.

David signs off;

*So bless you, lad*
*Yours ever*
*David Williamson*

# Max's Approach to Art

There are two seminal documents which give an insight into Max's heart and mind. One is his journal, which, while not an actual daily diary, gives a vivid feel for what his life was like at various periods. Its entries for his early days when he first went to art school are both interesting and entertaining. The other vital document is his *My Approach to Art.*

This essay consists partly of memoir, and partly of explanations and reflections. Intended to be one of three long records of his life, this middle one, written in 1958, is a wealth of information (the others were never completed or published).

It is mostly about the craft of painting but it also describes some of what he wrote and some of the music he enjoyed. A competent, fluent and thoughtful writer, Max outlines his personal history and gives readers a good idea of how and where he lived. As we know, he arrived at Birmingham as the Arts and Crafts Movement made famous by William Morris and John Ruskin was beginning to fade. In this period Max found much beauty in painting and decoration which he could benefit from and contribute to.

The Movement had been partly driven by Socialists, but although Max had grown up in a liberal and aware milieu, he could not be described as political. His focus was almost entirely directed to whatever painting or drawing was on the table or easel in front of him. Painting was his priority almost every time, and then writing. In essence, his creative approach was founded on reverence and even spirituality.

The other significant paper is Max's diary. His first entry, written on September 14th 1901, starts with a neatly written and clear Foreword quoted on page 38. The present writer has noted Max's wishes and has, of course, read his notes carefully – though Max might not have been expecting the (first) account of his story to be written by a woman.

A reader who embarks on *My Approach to Art* after *Crusaders* cannot fail to notice that, as discussed previously, the former contains a number of appreciative mentions of and warm comments about Connie, her achievements, and about the couple's working partnership. This happy situation does not seem to be mutual.

Although Connie was clearly fond of Max and was his wife and prime co-worker, his absence from Connie's text is noticeable. It is hard not to interpret this absence as an indicator that he valued her much more than she valued him, but this could be a false conclusion.

There are other surprising omissions. For example, Max hardly mentions the decorative artist Arthur Gaskin who was promoted to being a lecturer while still a student. Even more significantly, he says little about Joseph Southall. This man was the one who was a key influence on Max despite not actually being a member of the School's staff. He was particularly helpful to Max in respect of teaching him about tempera.

Gaskin used tempera, and was an illustrator of woodcuts for William Morris's Kelmscott Press. Like Max, he too profited from the company of his friend Joseph Southall.

Southall was a member of the Society of Friends. He lived in Edgbaston and attended Meeting at Bull Lane in Birmingham, but there is no indication that Maxwell went there either with him or on his own. Southall's *Corporation Street*, one of his large and dramatic paintings, is to be found prominently displayed in Birmingham Art Gallery. Max stated that he learned more from Southall than from any other artist, which makes it all the more surprising that he is not given attention, even if not prominence.

Max's *My Approach to Art* comments on much of what has already been described. But, he also wrote that he learned more and painted better paintings as he got older. He attributed this largely to his changed feelings after Connie's death. There were times when the two were the closest of couples, and their joint contribution to this world was to create art together, and in doing so (usually) value each other's opinion.

Diana Armfield kept an eye on Max after Connie's death:

*"I called on him whenever I could and invited him to Kew when he could spare the time. After some years, he not only got over the shock of losing her, but had a new lease of life in his work and sympathies, but he caused Harold much sorrow by continually over-spending and attempting to blame Harold … Harold was long suffering and wrote him long explanatory letters, but Max wouldn't understand them being, as he implied, occupied with higher thoughts!"*

# Max on His Own

Max soldiered on visiting galleries and exhibitions, continuing to observe and study. He must have felt very alone as he reflected on his life with Connie. Yes, there were many times when she had been difficult, but despite these, he must have missed her greatly. Happily, he was in touch with some family members as well as friends like Norman Silvester.

He had his painting. Despite a heart attack in 1953 he was keen to carry on working. In both domestic and artistic spheres, he had to create new routines and rituals. How difficult was this for him?

For decades, especially the latter ones, Max's purposes in life had been to paint, and to care for Connie, but now that she no longer needed him, perhaps he found that he no longer needed her. Or, that he was needing her in a different way.

He invited Stuart Armfield, his cousin, to come and stay and paint for several months, and that seemed to suit him much more than being on his own. They got on very well together.

However, after Connie's death Max had room to grow alone and differently. This was fuelled by reading more, visiting more exhibitions, and getting to grips with dynamic symmetry, a method of organising the composition of paintings according to specific mathematical and geometrical calculations. This was introduced to him by Professor Jay Hambidge, an influential teacher he met in the USA, who stressed to his students the importance of the compositional proportions of paintings. This system he was experimenting with derived from analysis of the works of ancient Greek and Egyptian artists, craftsmen and architects. Max was also keen on fibonacci, a numerical sequence which he sometimes used to guide how he composed his pictures, but which did not interest his niece Diana.

# Occult

In Tate Britain, in the archive containing numerous papers about Max's life, there are notebooks closely filled with his handwritten notes. Some of the writing is neat and taut, but some is not. The pages offer no respite to the eyes: there are no paragraphs and no gaps, but numerous underlinings, headings and quotations. Most of this text is in black ink, but some is in red. There are also simple, abstract little sketches. The words are not easy to read, but while one is questioning what they mean, one wants to know what is all this for? Who is Max writing for?

He wrote the words Law, Nirvana and Space, and Brahmanic Elements, Archetype or Sigil and phrases such as "purified enlightenment" and "elimination of the ego" but understanding his words and what they meant to him is not easy. He drew the signs of the planets and a variety of diagrams, such as those of Earth supporting Water supporting Fire, above which was Air and then Aether.

One clear piece of information that the notebooks revealed was that Max began to refer himself (not for the first time) by a new name: Mayananda. This could be explained by his connection to Ananda Coomraswamy, a unique Sri Lankan philosopher and historian who was an interpreter of Indian culture to the west. After some dipping into the texts, it is not clear who Max wanted or expected to use this name – other than himself.

The notebooks were in good condition, and it would seem that Max had just copied out phrases fluently and (usually) steadily without pausing. It was hard to know what to make of them and perhaps they can only be revealed or read to serious students of the occult – people like Max, who choose to be named Mayananda.

It is difficult to conclude other than that this student of the occult had written these for his own benefit. Perhaps Max was learning their contents by heart in order to gain knowledge, or copying them just because it pleased him to do so. Whatever the reason, the notebooks contain a great deal of work, care and meaning. He seems to be interested in Tarot, witchcraft, para-sciences and esoteric knowledge. Apparently, amongst the Tate's documents, there are letters showing that Max was in touch with others with similar interests, notably Aleister Crowley and Dion Fortune, though there is no suggestion that he met either of them. Both these two were magicians. The former, known as The

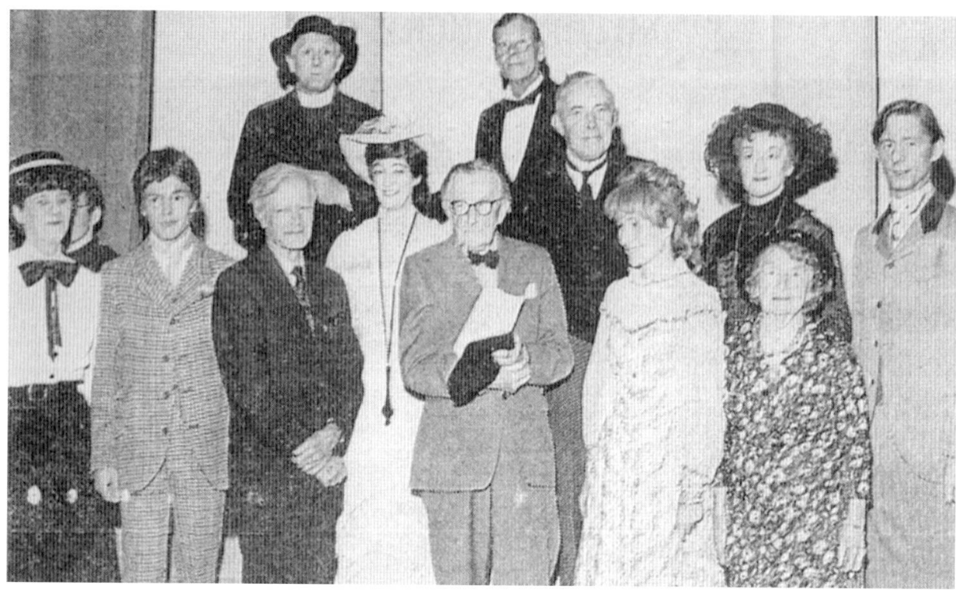

*Max on stage with the Cotswold Players.*

Wickedest Man in the World, founded a religion, wrote poetry and prose, painted and climbed mountains. The latter became a member of the Theosophical Society and of the Alpha and Omega Temple of the former Hermetic Order of the Golden Dawn, and co-founded a religion called The Fraternity of the Inner Light. The initial Quaker influences in Max's life seem a long, long way off.

It is hard to know what he was getting from his studies of the occult. And we cannot be sure of Max's reasons, although we know that when he made and did something he made and did it thoroughly. We know he researched a wide variety of things such as dynamic symmetry, Swinburne, and Italian artists.

Had Connie been interested in the occult? Perhaps she had, though she was very ill at the time when Max was already engaging more with his new interests. Did she read any of Max's theosophical and esoteric books? One does not know, but we should not forget that thirty or so years earlier, when she confided in Geoffrey Whitworth shortly before her marriage, she actually mentioned the word "occult" in connection with Maxwell.

# 58

# Alexander Ballard

At an unknown date, but around the time when he had been a widower for some time, Max experienced a crucial and positive change to his life. Through a mutual friend who needed accommodation, he met Alexander Ballard, the owner of a book shop. He seemed to go by two first names, Alexander and Arthur, varying which he used, as did others who knew him.

He and Max must have made a striking pair together, for Max – in size and figure – has been described as a sparrow, whereas Alexander was more of a solid and substantial build.

We do not know exactly when they met, but they developed a warm friendship initially founded on a shared appreciation of music. They both painted, and it seems likely that Alexander, who was younger, looked after Max as he (Max) entered his 80s and 90s, thus providing appropriate – but totally unlooked for – recompense for a man who had himself spent many years looking after someone else. Max did not write much about Alexander, so it has not been possible to find out any more details of his life and death other than that he seemed to move house often.

Alexander was much, much more than a carer, though caring came to be an important and essential part of what he did. He became Max's invaluable agent and critic as much as his companion, and his support buoyed Max up and encouraged him, thus enabling Max to carry on painting, and to improve his painting.

Max's final move was to Warminster, a town within sight of Wiltshire's gentle chalk hills. Teddington House – a large town house which he may have owned or, more probably, rented part of, was renovated in the 1960s. It is likely that Max was already ensconced by then but it is difficult to imagine that he could have paid for the renovation.

Alexander was an excellent travelling companion. In September 1960, he and Max went to France by train for two weeks, and Max kept a diary of their trip.

*"Pauline very kindly called for me at 7pm and we picked up A in Ringwood. He had had a hectic day but sold a large picture … We got off to time, a very rough and noisy crossing … banging etc and we didn't get much sleep.*

*From Havre we arranged to go 2nd with a couchette, the 2nds (Second Class) not nearly so good as ours but everything much more calm and 'sparse'. The landscape really so little changed in spite of all the bombing etc. I only saw one caravan all the way from Havre to Nice – and no bungalows."*

Alexander also helped Max with other creative projects, but this time they were literary ones. Most notable was *My Approach to Art,* mentioned previously. Taken as a whole, Max produced a very substantial and comprehensive body of writing in his long life.

It is in this essay that he describes *how* he paints, and his search for ways to improve his work. For example, he struggled to understand why he liked certain aspects of it, and he reported periods of frustration and dissatisfaction.

Travelling proved to be a significant stimulus to Max's work. In Italy he wrote, *"Painting a good deal in the parks and streets, I began to appreciate more modern painting."*

Max described the period in the USA in far more detail than Connie did. He wrote about landscape, American organisations, writing articles, painting a large mural, and he noted that *"All this varied experience gave me confidence and breadth which indeed the whole of my seven years in America accentuated."* He also wrote a book entitled *The Artist in America.*

# 59

# A Glimpse Across Constance's Career

In 1929, as has been mentioned, Connie wrote *Crusaders,* her reminiscences. Her unique career – if career is the right word for her uneven and innovative trajectory through life – was initially founded on writing. Indeed, almost everything she did involved writing. She wrote literary texts, scripts, reports, appeals, talks, proposals, articles, letters and so on. She wrote for the Cotswold Players, for Greenleaf and in order to explain her theories about acting and teaching. Her practical activities such as writing and directing plays and pageants were joined with ones such as music, dancing, and embroidery. Nearly everything was written down at some point.

She was also involved with the Women's Movement. Although of course she espoused the women's cause, she seems to have been less involved with demonstrations and meetings than her sister Di. But she was certainly the friend of suffragettes. And, importantly, she was probably best-known as the founder of the Lyceum Club. In the early 1900s, when a young woman, she had the vision, energy and skill to encourage her friends to want to help her create a special club. Its founding led to the establishment of other clubs in other countries. Its aims were serious and ambitious, and it thrived for a good thirty years. Years later it revived itself, and the International Association of Lyceum Clubs now has clubs in about twenty countries.

Quite rightly, Connie was proud of her achievements.

# A Glimpse Across Maxwell's Career

Looking down a list of Max's paintings, and taking into account others which are dispersed around galleries, private homes and public buildings – making a total of some hundreds – one sees clearly the breadth and quantity of what he created. He painted portraits, figures, scenes in America and Italy, still lifes, landscapes and "mystical" subjects. As well as tempera, he used oils and watercolours. In size, some of his work is on board, some on canvas, some on card. The paintings range from about 76 x 25cms to just over 12 x 12cms. Most are signed with his monogram. The earliest were painted in 1900, the last ones in 1970. He painted wherever he found himself, preferring privacy and lack of distraction. He also illustrated books (his own and those of others). He painted about four hours a day, and usually worked on several pictures simultaneously. And he played and composed music. Quite some routine.

Max's first exhibition was at The Paris Salon, and his last at The Fine Arts Society in New Bond Street, and the time between those points had few gaps and was studded with other (almost annual) exhibitions. It is an amazing output.

Happily, Max had two prestigious and successful exhibitions at The Fine Art Society in London as his life neared its end. Then followed his paintings in exhibitions entitled Homage to Bach, Homage to Jean Clouet (a miniature painter), and Homage to the Oriental Masters. These last ones were Homage to Maxwell Armfield, April and May 1970, and 90th Birthday Exhibition, September and October 1971.

The Introduction to the first of these by Alexander Ballard was both comprehensive and informative, but it was probably Max who decided on the striking front cover of the catalogue. Against a cream background it has a bold image in black, brown and white, the three capital letters I, A ad O, and three wings which symbolise lightness and spirituality. Apparently it draws its title from the Kabbalistic identities of Isis, Apophis and Osiris, and is connected to the Hermetic Order of the Golden Dawn. Max would have chosen those images with care.

And, in September 1973, after his death, his work was exhibited in a Memorial Exhibition of Designs, Drawings and Watercolours.

Alexander Ballard, Max's firmest companion at this stage, was well aware of the years, if not decades, of esoteric study that Max had undertaken. He noted that his (Max's) painting had by now become inextricably connected to his writing and musical composition.

Max published two books under his assumed name. These were *Tarot for Today* and *The Wonder Beyond.*

In his late eighties Max was appointed as a Vice-President of the Cotswold Players. He accepted this despite stating that he had no idea what Vice-Presidents were for, *"except to rake in money."*

Patrick Howell, the chronicler of the Players, wrote, *"It was normal practice to write to each of the Vice-Presidents annually to ask them for their 5 guinea fee for being a VP."*

Apparently Max answered the request thus:

*"I sent a small donation last year but I did not intend it to be an annual one. I think there is some little misunderstanding and I don't remember anything about the vice-presidency of the CP. Unfortunately I cannot get over to see your shows as I no longer have the car, but I am glad to see that you are flourishing and send you my best wishes, of course."*

We cannot tell from this whether Alexander was around. If he was not, everyday life may well have been less easy for Max, and companionship certainly less available. Also, Max still found both travelling and managing money difficult. Despite all this, he is still remembered fondly by the Cotswold Players with whom he and Connie worked for sixty years. The theatre continues to thrive.

And, in September 1973, after his death, his work was exhibited in a Memorial Exhibition of Designs, Drawings and Watercolours. Its Introduction, written by Alexander Ballard, was both comprehensive and informative, and the exhibition was a great success.

# Max's Last Letters

Exchanging letters was one of Max's pleasures, and one which he enjoyed almost to the end of his life. In July 1971, only months before he died, he wrote the following letter to Diana and Bernard. He was obviously reflecting on members of the Armfield family and their interest in flowers:

*Dear Diana and Bernard,*

*It was so nice to get your letter – so few people now write letters, and being so isolated here they are doubly welcome. I suppose it is one of the inevitable results of age as one becomes more and more immobile it is so difficult to keep contact with people, who, in any case are too busy to live. Diana's peregrinations of the garden are quite delightful: it is odd how this <u>flower</u> attraction persists all through the family in various ways. It is I believe, hereditary and came from my (Armfield) grandmother – so devoted to them, as I remember, Gfather had green fingers and of course, was a devoted gardener.*

The following extract was taken from a letter Max wrote in April 1969, after one of Bernard's books had just been published. It is evidence of his determination to keep going and his continuing interest in others:

*Dear Bernard,*

*So many thanks for sending your <u>excellent</u> book and no less for including my 2 in it – really very kind of you – as of course they are not really your shaped palette!*

*I think it is fascinating that whilst your attitude is almost a direct antithesis of mine yet I very much appreciate and admire – what I – now at any rate – could not at all do.*

*I think your colour is quite lovely and of course that really depends on all the other facets you deal with so directly and clearly. I love the kitchen table with Alexander's lemon and of course the mushrooms and quince of lemon.*

And here is another late but warm and poignant letter:

*Dear Diana, 5.21.70 (sic) from 9 Abbey Churchyard, Bath*

*Thanks for your letter. Actually Arthur asked about that ms as he is doing an introduction for my catalogue and I thought he might get some dope from it (my memory re. dates etc is now non-existent). So I <u>would</u> like it, please – this sort of interest in the late nineties etc is bringing a lot of ancient stuff into evidence (one's sins always catch up with one eventually etc etc.) Yes, I go on turning them out. … so am kept ticking over and supremely grateful to be able to tick as long as I have to be around.*

Max died in Teddington House in Warminster in 1972. While Connie's golden sphere attracts certain attention, Max's house is situated almost opposite a different and less prominent feature: a plain grey obelisk, topped with a pineapple and an urn. This was erected to mark the occasion of the enclosure of the parish in 1783. It suits Max better than the golden orb, for it is just there, planted firmly in the heart of a country town, serving as a reminder to local people of an important event which, on the whole, disadvantaged many of them. But it has a quiet elegance.

I have, so far, been unable to find out exactly where Max was buried.

# Epilogue

Connie and Max, the main characters in this book, were well travelled. Between them they lived or stayed in places as widespread as California and the Cotswolds, Southampton and Sheffield, Polperro and Paris. My father David went to some of them too. Though he had a minor role and was in fewer scenes, I believe he earned his place in the main story.

Think of the three people as actors, embarking on a play. Their personal life scripts were sometimes influenced by other plays or authors as well as each other. Sometimes there was the chance to rehearse, sometimes not. At times they read script-in-hand or even improvised. Things were not always perfect, but they often created and came across hope and beauty.

Music, dance, and the natural world added to the lives of Max, Connie and David, as did events set in cities, on beaches or in forests. Keen to live to the full, these actors stretched their hands towards their audiences.

They travelled between now and then, raising thoughts about what had happened and what might happen. At times they did this alone, at times with others. Sometimes they waited to be invited, sometimes they dived straight into life's mêlée.

The story of Connie and Max and David is essentially about communication, for each reached out in their own way. As the years passed they created joy and helped each other – and others – to explore their lives fully, to move forward and to bring warmth to those they met.

# Connie's Books

The following titles are of most of Connie's books, of which some are fiction, some non-fiction:

**Fiction**

*The April Princess*; Cassell, 1903
*The Boudoir Critic*, 1903
*For Heart o'Gold*; Harpers, 1904
*Conflict*; Constable, 1907
*The Daughter*; Constable, 1908
*The June Princess*; Chatto, 1909
*Mothers and Fathers*; Chatto, 1912
*Commoners' Rights*; Chatto, 1912
*New Wine and Old Bottles*; Fisher Unwin, 1913
*Una and the Lions*; Chatto, 1914
*On the Fighting Line*; Putnam, 1915
*Redwing*; Allen and Unwin, 1916
*The Unholy Experiment*; Chatto, 1924
*Justice Walk*; Allen and Unwin, 1924

**Childrens' books**

*The Wizards of Ryetown*; (Hurst and Blackett), 1905
*The Flower Book*; Chatto (Warne USA), 1918
*Sylvia's Travels*; Dent (Dutton USA), 1911
*Wonder Tales of the World*; (Harcourt Brace USA), 1920
*The Armfield's Animal Book*; Duckworth (Harcourt Brace USA), 1922
*Tales from Timbuktu*; Chatto (Harcourt Brace USA), 1923
*The Blue Bus Route*; OUP, 1927

## Sociological

*Woman – A Few Shrieks*; Garden City Press, 1907
*The Wings of a Dove*; Headley Bros, 1914
*Crusaders*; Duckworth, 1929

## Plays

*The Curious Herbal*
*The Gilded Wreath*
*On the Fighting Line*
*Belle and Beau*
*Oranges and Beans*
*Crusaders, Reminiscences*; Duckworth, 1929

# Works Exhibited

The following list of titles gives a sample of the work Max exhibited at the Homage exhibition:

*Je Pars Peut-être Demain*
*Salome*
*Truth*
*The Artist's Mother*
*Keith Henderson*
*Percy Grainger*
*Portrait Of Alexander Ballard 1965*
*Ice Plant On the Hudson*
*Central Park, New York*
*Grey Owl*
*Pot Of Delft*
*Breakfast On The Farm*
*Gentian In A Shell*
*Mountain Miniature*
*Quinces*
*The Chinese Lotus*
*Cotswold*
*The Great Mirror*
*Cyprus At El Tovar, Grand Canyon*
*Tarot: Trump IX*
*Prometheus*
*Day – Evening*
*Proud Galleons*
*I Saw Three Ships*
*Red Tape and Sealing Wax*

*Appendix 3*

# Maxwell's Paintings and Publications

A selection of Maxwell's paintings and publications:

*An Artist in America*, 1925
*An Artist in Italy*, 1926
*Tempera Painting Today*, 1946
*Manual of Tempera Painting*, 1930
*Stencil Printing*, 1927
*American Stage Designs*, 1919
*Rhythmic Shape*, 1920

# Bibliography

I have been helped by several books, particularly *Above the Battlefield*, Grace Brockington, Yale University Press, 2010 and *Consistently Brilliant on a Breezy Hilltop,* Patrick Howell, Quicksilver Publications, 2016 and *A Life Force in Life Science* Penny Freedman, Book Guild Ltd., 2020. I also benefitted from *The Amazing and Preposterous Constance Smedley* (unpublished) by Frank Hatt.

# Books by the same author

**Fiction (novels)**

*The Estuary*
*The Reed Flute*
*Companion to Owls*
*As Best We Can*

**Non-fiction**

*Prisons of Promise*
*The Curious Mr Howard*
*In the Wake of War*
*Lady Sue Ryder of Warsaw*

Find out more at: *www.tessawest.co.uk*